AF291498

ILEANA
OF
ROMANIA

ILEANA OF ROMANIA

Princess, Exile and Mother Superior

THOM NICKELS

FONTHILL

First published in Great Britain in 2026 by
Fonthill
An imprint of
Pen & Sword Books Ltd
Yorkshire – Philadelphia
www.fonthill.media

ISBN 978-1-03615-643-5

Typeset in SabonLTStd 11.5/14.5 by
SJmagic DESIGN SERVICES, India.
Printed and bound in the UK by CPI Group (UK) Ltd, Croydon, CR0 4YY

The Publisher's authorised representative in the EU for product
safety is Authorised Rep Compliance Ltd., Ground Floor,
71 Lower Baggot Street, Dublin D02 P593, Ireland.
www.arccompliance.com

For a complete list of Pen & Sword titles please contact
PEN & SWORD BOOKS LIMITED
George House, Units 12 & 13, Beevor Street, Off Pontefract Road,
Barnsley, South Yorkshire, S71 1HN, England
E-mail: enquiries@pen-and-sword.co.uk
Website: www.pen-and-sword.co.uk

or

PEN AND SWORD BOOKS
1950 Lawrence Rd, Havertown, PA 19083, USA
E-mail: uspen-and-sword@casematepublishers.com
Website: www.penandswordbooks.com

This book is dedicated to Mother Elizabeth—Carol Klipa
Bacha—an Orthodox nun and founder of the
Christmas Monastery School and New Tikhvin Skete
of the Holy Mother of God in Palm Coast, Florida,
and to the memory of Christine Arentz of
Boston and Colorado.

Acknowledgements

Almost a decade ago, I attempted to visit Romania as a travel writer by filling out forms provided for me by the Ministry of Tourism of Romania. It was a cumbersome process, made even stranger when I heard nothing from the ministry after submission. Later, I was told the political situation in Romania was rocky and not to expect a reply. Years later, I purchased Princess Ileana's book, *I Live Again*, not knowing what prompted me to do so but nevertheless feeling drawn to find out about the woman. Little did I know the stage was being set for a message from Mother Elizabeth in Palm Coast, Florida—whom I did not know—who said she had something interesting to discuss and would I please give her a call. That call set off plans to do this book after the Florida nun told me she had worked with Princess Ileana—Mother Alexandra—for many years and was privy to many of her secrets that she had never published in books or official texts.

Andrei Nicolau of Compass Travel Romania LLC, a Romanian tour operator, worked patiently with me for months mapping out a respectable road trip itinerary (with a talented tour guide) throughout the western and northern parts of the country.

The good nuns at the Monastery of the Transfiguration, especially Mother Christophora, were very helpful in aiding my research.

Contents

Monasticism and Royalty

The hard truth that a man determined to give his life to God will never contest is that every priest who does not tend to Sanctity is really, rigorously, absolutely, a Judas and a piece of filth.

—Leon Bloy

The decision to leave secular life and enter the monastic life—a life far simpler filled with personal restrictions many would call "repressive and unhealthy"—would be a monumental one for most people. And yet throughout history, many people—including royals—have taken this step and changed their lives without looking back. This sort of renunciation, or the walking away from a comfortable life to voluntarily embrace what, by comparison, may be seen as a life of solitude and harshness, occurs within the confines of many religious traditions.

The left-wing *Guardian* newspaper, for instance, often highlights men who have retreated from their roles as powerful CEOs to become Buddhist monks in obscure monasteries. "From CEO-to-Buddhist-monk" features are far more popular than Christian monastic narratives because the secular world feels more comfortable with dogma-free Buddhism—with its emphasis on generic meditation—than it does with traditional Christianity, especially Catholicism and Eastern Orthodoxy.

The so-called monastic personality—if one even dares to coin such a term—is a definite type. In meeting a Buddhist and a Catholic monk together, one might see striking similarities in behavior and an inward holiness or spirituality that shines through most everything the monks say and do.

In 1958, Tudor Edwards wrote in *Worlds Apart: A Journey to the Great Living Monasteries of Europe*, that:

> Your first encounter with a monk is a curious experience. You look upon him with something approaching awe and a deep curiosity. Your imagination vests him with supernatural qualities, with the power of sustained prayer and contemplation, with a mysticism that almost removes him from human kind. Or perhaps, like a certain school of novelists, you see him as an escapist or a refugee, a disillusioned lover, a discharged bankrupt or an ex-criminal who wishes to atone.

Edwards goes on to say that "It is most unlikely that he is any of these things," and of course that would be correct.

"As a guest in a monastery you will be privileged to share to a large extent in the life of the community," Edwards writes. "There is in the Luxembourg Museum of Paris a painting by Dauban showing a stranger being received by a convent, and it is a poignant interpretation of the fifty-third chapter of the Rule of St. Benedict. Your cell is little different from those of the monks, perhaps it is that of a monk, you dine with the community in the refectory, and the day, according to how you are disposed, may be bounded by the same canonical hours. There are few limitations, few exactments other than those dictated by your own conscience. At times you may even feel an intruder in this community of dedicated men. You know that their austerity is absolute, yours is softened by dispensations. Passing them in the cloisters you instinctively edge close to the wall, as do the novices in France. It is a world of intoned voices and Latin texts, of bells and plainsong, and of protracted silences, and there are the odors of incense, guttering candles, starched linen, wax polish, the dampness of ancient stone, stale food, feet, of men alone...

> In English monasteries in the middle of the afternoon there is a welcome bowl of tea, known as caritas, and here again the monks drift in and out of the refectory, each standing in silence as he drinks with two hands firmly holding the bowl. After vespers a guest may well retire to the library, which has always an intriguing, sometimes

celebrated collection of books, for a monastery without a library is a fortress without an arsenal.

Death is nothing in a monastery. It is indeed often almost eagerly awaited in the spirit of the old martyrs, and when it comes it is the easiest and most gradual of change-overs, the great day of deliverance—the janua caeli or door of Eternal Life. And yet, as a Scottish priest observed in the same monastic parlour, "Death is a terrible thing, ugly, painful and unnatural because the soul is torn from the body." In a sense, however, these monks have already died, and their existence here is simply a purifying ablutionary process.

Worlds Apart is not about women's monasteries, because in the 1950s there could have been a real problem regarding access to women's monasteries, comparable perhaps to the rules surrounding the prohibition of women on Mount Athos, the center of monasticism in the Orthodox Christian world. And yet examples of women changing their lives and entering Christian monasteries after years of marriage, children, and grandchildren, are not uncommon. The life of Mother Alice-Elizabeth, a Greek Orthodox nun who was formerly Princess Alice of Battenberg, is one such case.

Born in February 1885 in the Tapestry Room at Windsor Castle, this great-granddaughter of Queen Victoria was given the title Her Serene Highness, Princess of Battenberg. Queen Victoria dictated the infant be called Alice. Alice was born with congenital deafness and had great difficulty pronouncing words throughout her childhood. Her parents, Princess Victoria and Prince Louis of Battenberg, taught young Alice to lip-read, but in the end this was not enough.

Author and theologian Archbishop Chrysostomos writes in his book *A Greek Orthodox Nun in Buckingham Palace*:

In effect, her deafness was to some extent a lifelong deficit. This fact is said to have disquieted Queen Elizabeth, the Queen Mother of England who considered Princess Alice handicapped … Princess Alice became very proficient in a number of languages, lip reading and speaking English, German, French, and, in later life, modern Greek.

Her married life began in 1902, when she met Prince Andrew of Greece when she was 17 years old. A romance blossomed, and one year later their engagement was announced. They settled in Athens in the Greek Royal Palace and had four daughters—Princess Margarita, Princess Theodora, Princess Cecilie, and Princess Sophie. Their only son, Prince Philip, married Queen Elizabeth II, who died in 2022.

Baptized a Lutheran as an infant, Princess Alice converted to Orthodox Christianity in October 1928 in a small chapel in a suburb of Paris. Prince Andrew died in 1944 in Monaco. In 1949, the princess became the subject of world headlines when it was reported that Prince Philip's mother was living as a nun.

She had gone to the Greek isle of Tinos, where her intention was to start a sisterhood of monastic nurses. As Mother Alice-Elizabeth, she had been given the freedom by the famous Church of the Virgin to design her own grey nun's habit and to structure her own religious order. The church houses the miraculous icon of the All-Holy-Mother of God, one of Greece's most popular places of pilgrimage. As Archbishop Chrysostomos notes, her religious habit was of her own design, and her life was marked by controversy, some of it brought about by her bouts of mental illness and her staunch advocacy of the restoration of the female deaconate in the Greek Orthodox Church. Prelates accused her of "Protestantism," and many Orthodox clerics referred to her as "a so-called nun." She died in December 1969 in Buckingham Palace, where Queen Elizabeth had given her large rooms. Always a chain-smoker, Mother Alice-Elizabeth would wander the halls of the palace smoking her Woodbine cigarettes.

Archbishop Chrysostomos adds:

Mother Alice-Elizabeth, mocked in the popular British press as "the royal who had a habit," "the chain-smoking, card-playing nun," the "mad princess who had a habit," and other witless, insulting epithets in that style, was, in fact, as her relative, Mother Alexandra, the former Princess Ileana of Romania and Archduchess of Austria described her in our personal discussions, a woman who suffered from a nervous breakdown and overcame it; and a deeply religious, spiritual, and otherwise worldly woman who derived strength from her Orthodox Faith and ignored those, some from her own family, who misunderstood her and maligned her. Mother Alexandra very sincerely confessed her immense admiration for Mother

Alice-Elizabeth as someone who faced adversity with humility and who had an instinctual love ... for the poor and for society's so-called outcasts.

In yet another royal-to-monastic story from history, Grand Duchess Elizabeth, the sister of Tsarina Alexandra, Empress of Russia, wife of Tsar Nicholas II, and Mother Alice-Elizabeth's aunt, entered monastic life after the assassination of her husband, Grand Duke Sergei Alexandrovich, the son of Russian Tsar Alexander II and Empress Maria Alexandrovna. A socialist revolutionary threw a bomb into Alexandrovich's carriage in February 1905, killing him and splintering his body into pieces. Because Elizabeth knew that her husband had been responsible for the expulsion of 200,000 Jews from Russia, she saw the murder as a sort of cosmic revenge. She then decided to spend the rest of her life in repentance and devote herself to the service of God by becoming a monastic and establishing a nursing sisterhood devoted to the poor.

Elizabeth was killed by the Bolsheviks in 1918 one day after her sister, Tsarina Alexandra, her husband Nicholas, and five children were executed by the provisional government. The Grand Duchess and seven other Romanovs were beaten to death and their bodies thrown down a mine shaft.

Lenin himself commented on the Grand Duchess's murder when he said, "Virtue with the crown on is a greater enemy to the world revolution than a hundred tyrant tsars."

Chrysostomos writes that both Mother Elizabeth ("Ella") and Mother Alice-Elizabeth were accused of not being "real" nuns. In Mother Elizabeth's case, it was because she did not establish a sisterhood after a long life of strict ascetic discipline and practice. This despite the fact that the Grand Duchess was canonized a saint in 1981 by the Russian Orthodox Church Outside Russia, and again in 1992 by the Moscow Patriarchate. She remains one of the most beloved saints in Russia.

Entering the silence

Remember that the best of prayers are not made with words, but with desire alone.

—Jacques Maritain

The journals of Trappist monk Thomas Merton, author of the bestselling book *The Seven Storey Mountain*, were written shortly after Merton entered the monastery of Our Lady of Gethsemani in Louisville, Kentucky, at the age of 26. Merton, who was born in France and educated in England, originally wanted to be a novelist when he migrated to New York City to resume his studies at Columbia. Merton's life on Perry Street in Greenwich Village was typical of that of many young bohemians of the era: bar hopping, cafes, women, bookstores, films, and other intellectual pursuits. This life soon paled for the budding mystic.

The Seven Storey Mountain chronicles Merton's conversion to Catholicism and his decision to become a monk. He first applied to the Franciscan Order, but the vocation director there rejected him because he admitted that he had once gotten a girl pregnant. The Trappists, however, were willing to look the other way. Until the day he died—December 10, 1968—Merton (Father Louis) was never what some call a sanctimonious Holy Roller but a man subject to all sorts of temptations. As a seasoned monk, he drank beer, read Lenny Bruce and Nietzsche, and defended the poetry of Allen Ginsberg.

Merton became a monk in the years before Vatican II, when Catholicism had a more traditional cast. Vatican II changed many things in Catholic life, especially the rubrics of the Mass. Merton was ambivalent about some of these changes. In his journal he notes:

Catholic Aggiornamento: A priest is amazed that some of his people continue to say the Rosary at Mass. He announces a special service. Sunday evening all are to bring Rosaries and candles ... walk in procession to a spot outside the Church where they will find a hole has been dug. They are to throw their rosaries in the hole. Spirit of liberty of Vatican II.

Merton, in this instance, sounds like Archbishop Lefebvre, who founded the Society of St. Pius X in 1970 in Écône, Switzerland, a canonical Catholic group championing the Latin Mass and in opposition to many of the innovations of the Second Vatican Council (1962–65).

In the mid-Sixties, Merton had a major crisis involving monastic celibacy. This life-changing experience occurred when he underwent an operation in a Louisville hospital and befriended a young nurse. Merton wrote:

> I remember being fed by a nurse at my first meal ... then trying to eat one myself and picking a small piece of veal off a plate with my fingers and sticking it in my mouth.

His relationship with the nurse, known in the journals as "M." (Margie), evolved into a romantic obsession. The world-famous monk-author suddenly found himself sneaking around the monastery late at night in order to make hushed phone calls to his beloved. In May 1966 he wrote:

> The trouble is that with M. and me it is not a game ... Humanly speaking the situation is impossible. We are terribly in love, and it goes very deep, perhaps more even with her than with me.

Other journal entries make him sound like a lovesick adolescent: "She is the sweetest person I have ever known."

At other times he comes off like a hippie at Woodstock: "We [M.] ate herring and ham (not very much eating!) and drank our wine and read poems and talked of ourselves and mostly made love and love and love for five hours."

Merton was able to spend time with M. because the abbot, Dom James, with whom he did not get along, gave him permission to live as a hermit in a small house on monastery grounds. Flocks of visitors found their way to his door. The Berrigan brothers, poet Denise Levertov, Wendell Berry, and Joan Baez came knocking, while random tourists would show up uninvited. Religious fanatics sought him out to tell him their dreams or that his life was in danger. On more than one occasion, Merton found himself hiding behind a tree to avoid the religious paparazzi, similar to those who would come to Mother Alexandra's Orthodox monastery in Ellwood City, Pennsylvania, hoping to catch a glimpse of Romanian royalty, the former Princess Ileana—great-granddaughter of Queen Victoria— who became a monastic after raising her family and being forced to leave her native Romania after expulsion by the communists in 1948, the topic of this book.

Merton in many ways was the Catholic version of the Dalai Lama. Living in the hermitage apart from the monastery gave him freedoms denied the other monks: he could ditch his habit for work clothes and escape to downtown Louisville with friends to grab lunch (and beer) at a favorite eatery, then come back and change back into his habit again.

In June 1966, he wrote: "I realize that what is most wrong in my relationship with M. now is that I no longer trust her fully." In fact, a close friend of Merton's at this point tells him to forget M. because she is "narcissistic, selfish, and not capable of loving another human being." Their relationship continues, however.

In the journals, Merton continues to think about Catholic renewal:

> There is too much spite, envy, pettiness, savagery, and again too much of a brutal and arrogant spirit in this so called Catholic renewal: too much conceit and hubris, and in the end the same old authoritarian and intolerant ways in a new form.

He also writes about the "incredible number" of men leaving the monastery, especially the Trappist monastery in California. Throughout the world, soon after the close of the Vatican Council there was an exodus of monks and nuns from convents and seminaries.

Merton's eclectic reading habits at this time include writers like Faulkner, Sartre, and Camus. He also becomes more interested in Zen. Intense pangs of conscience continue to torment him when it comes to M., and his battles with Dom James, the abbot, plunge to a new low. Merton describes the abbot as "the very incarnation of New England middle class, efficiency loving, thrifty, crafty, operating, sanctimonious religiosity." Naturally, when Dom James eventually discovers Merton's affair with M.—this happens when a (younger) monk who drove Merton to Louisville to meet M. spills the beans—there is hell to pay.

When singer Joan Baez visits, she and Merton picnic on the hermitage lawn.

We talked of my love for M. and I read some of the poems and
Joan was ready to drive ninety miles an hour through the rain to
Cincinnati so I could see M. when she got off at the hospital.

After another struggle with his conscience, Merton breaks ties with
M., then changes his mind again: "Yesterday I had to go to Louisville
for a bursitis shot in the elbow. M. and I had arranged with Jim
Wygal that we would borrow his office and get together there, which
we did with a bottle of champagne." M. and Merton talk about
marriage but their plans never materialize. Merton realizes he is a
monk "through and through" and that he must end the affair. When
Dom James finds out about M., the boom is lowered.

Merton complains:

Meanwhile, I have to accept the punishment the Abbot is giving
me. Nothing great in itself, really, only his scorn and his narrow-
mindedness bearing down on me more directly, cutting off liberties
and what were really privileges—so I cannot truly complain.

M. was not Merton's first romantic temptation. John Cooney
writes that in 1963, three years before Merton met M., his dormant
sexuality was shaken by a beatnik tourist claiming to be a distant
relative but who was really a nymphomaniac. Merton said the
woman "gave me a wild time—a real battle, at times physical, and
finally when I got away alive and with most of my virtue intact
(I hope) I felt shaken, sick and scared."

When the relationship with M. was finally over, Merton burned
all of her letters, although he was haunted by her memory for some
time. He continued to dream about her and was even tempted to
call her while in Louisville on doctor's visits. Occasionally he found
solace in Schlitz beer:

So I go and get another beer. The supply is already running out.
I only had five cans. It is a hot night. Where will I be when the dark
falls and the dragons come and there is no more beer?

Mother Alice-Elizabeth might have felt similarly walking the
hallways of Buckingham Palace, chain-smoking her cigarettes.

Cooney says that at this time of his life, Merton resembled a well-fed Friar Tuck, rather than the pale, ascetic he was on ordination day. Cooney adds: "Now bald-headed, he looked like Pablo Picasso."

Merton begins to question everything. He writes about transferring to a Trappist monastery in Chile or New Mexico. His interest in Zen and Buddhism intensifies so that he begins to quote Chinese masters and non-Christian scripture as often as he quotes Christian saints. He also comes down hard on his brother monks:

> The fact is that this community is full of half-sick people, immensely vulnerable, wasting their lives in petty, neurotic machinations—and one simply does not needle such people. It does no good, and it encourages their sickness.

Although he is invited to religious conferences all over the world, Dom James says no to virtually every request.

Merton prays for strength under pressure. "I kneel down by the bed and look up at the icon of the nativity. The soft shaded light plays over the shelves of the Buddhist books in the silent bedroom." In another entry, he goes completely bawdy:

> The other day I was in town. It embarrasses me. Of course, I had to see the proctologist and that is always embarrassing—with your head down and your asshole up in the air, trying to talk about Mexican Indians.

When Dom James announces his retirement and when a new abbot is elected, Merton experiences a sense of elation. He is given a green light to travel to conferences in San Francisco and then to a series of conferences in the Far East, where he will meet with the Dalai Lama, tour Buddhist monasteries, and meet other Catholic clergy. It is in the Far East where his life will end suddenly.

His unexpected death was reported on the front page of *The New York Times*.

According to Cooney,

> The end, in fact, came at a conference cottage in Samutprakarn, some 20 miles from the Thai capital, on December 10th after he addressed

fellow monks at 10.45am on Marxism and Monastic Perspectives. Looking stressed, he retired for a shower. That afternoon he was found lying on his back with a five-foot fan which had landed diagonally across his body.

Merton wrote more than seventy books, most of them on spirituality and social issues.

Two monasteries quite contrary

The meal consisted of beans swimming in cold, oily water, and some cod-fish accompanied by a tepid oily sauce and celery. In addition each person received a loaf of brown bread, a pewter can full of excellent wine and a handful of raw garlic. The monks ate the latter in enormous quantities with apparent relish.
—Ralph. H. Brewster, *The 6,000 Beards of Athos*

Walking through a grand monastery such as St. Vincent Archabbey in Latrobe, Pennsylvania, at 8 a.m. on a snowy morning and seeing twenty-some seminarians practicing saying Mass might make you pause, as it did me, to ponder the beauty of it all. Though the Chapel of St. Gregory where the seminarians were practicing has a modernist design, it has traditional elements and is not ugly in the way far too many desacralized modern churches seem to be. A large crucifix hangs suspended above the candle-adorned altar, and though there are no side altars—a statue of the Virgin Mary can be seen off to the side— the space retains a traditional feeling, unlike the grand altar in the monastery's main basilica, which invokes the sterility of Bauhaus architecture.

The basilica's high altar was removed in 1954, and then came the removal of numerous side altars at which priests said private Masses. Still, this vast empty space does have a kind of beauty: large, white, marble statues of saints set against the side-aisle arches recall certain Roman-period rooms in the Philadelphia Museum of Art. And yet, while attending Mass and daily prayers there, my eyes often drifted to the apse, where the former high altar used to be, now filled with small chairs and, in this season, a large, albeit beautiful Christmas tree. By contrast, the Basilica of SS Peter and Paul in

Philadelphia kept its high altar, including the ornate baldacchino, and side altars intact after Vatican II. Monastery churches, however, tended to be subject to radical design innovations that pushed the envelope.

In 1846, a Benedictine monk named Boniface Wimmer arrived at St. Vincent with eighteen monks. The group hailed from Bavaria, and their mission was to establish churches and schools. After Wimmer was installed as pastor of St. Vincent in October of that year, he went on to establish the first Benedictine monastery, college, and seminary in North America. Ground was broken on St. Vincent de Paul (Minor) Basilica in 1891. It took fourteen years to build. St. Gregory's chapel was designed by Fr. Vincent Crosby, a graduate of Philadelphia's Tyler School of Art and a member of the Benedictine community since 1967. His international reputation as a designer of liturgical vestments for priests, bishops, popes, and even the Archbishop of Canterbury is well deserved. His studio, a few minutes' walk from the main monastery, contains a vast collection of framed, icon-like images of saints, as well as vestments and copes that are simultaneously contemporary and traditional.

Another of Fr. Crosby's creations, the monastery mausoleum, of which he was the architect, is perhaps the most stunning space in the monastery complex. Icons lighted by candles mark the entrance, and once through the doors of the rotunda, you come face-to-face with an Italian-marble replica of Michelangelo's Pietà surrounded by candles and a massive, Crosby-designed stained-glass window showing the risen Christ. On the walls are hand-carved Stations of the Cross, which the artist-monk found in the monastery bascment. Each station is labeled in German. These heavily detailed works of art feature three-dimensional silver helmets on the heads of the Roman soldiers.

St. Vincent is a thriving complex: it includes a seminary; the college of St. Vincent; separate dining rooms for seminarians, monks, and students; and a guesthouse complete with servers and menu ordering as found in any restaurant. The St. Vincent Fred Rogers Center for Early Learning and Children's Media is also within the complex. Mr. Rogers, a Presbyterian minister and close friend of the monastery, was a frequent visitor. The town of Latrobe is also the home of Rolling Rock beer.

I sat with the monks during Lauds, Vespers, and Compline, the three sets of prayers arranged throughout the day. These prayers involve the recitation and singing of the psalms, the overall effect of which is powerful, at one point causing my eyes to tear up. Daily Mass was reverent yet simple, with no incense or bells at consecration, much like the Jesuit Masses at St. Joseph's Catholic Church in Philadelphia's Old City.

I took the liberty of asking a monk if incense is ever used at Mass, because the liturgy seemed scaled down. "Occasionally, yes," he replied. "If I had my way, I would have incense at every Mass. But that's the way they want it here."

This is not to disparage the beauty of St. Vincent's. As an Orthodox Christian, I am used to certain ceremonials, and when I don't see them in Catholic liturgies, my usual reaction is to wonder why so many Catholic clergy want their liturgies to resemble mainstream Protestant worship services. Perhaps I want Catholicism to be like the Catholicism of my childhood and not like the Catholicism of the "new age," in which tradition is often cast aside to make way for innovations.

Yet Benedictine monasteries that are closely aligned to tradition do exist, such as Clear Creek Monastery in Oklahoma and Our Lady of Guadalupe Monastery in Silver Springs, New Mexico, where the Traditional Latin Mass is celebrated. In fact, while having my St. Benedict Medal blessed by the superior of the monastery's Oblates of St. Benedict (I belong to a Philadelphia-based community of ecumenical Oblates that permits Orthodox and other non-Catholic Christians to join), I learned that some of the monks at St. Vincent's contemplated going to Clear Creek, where the monks are very traditional.

The monks at St. Vincent's are members of the American-Cassinese Congregation. Many are foreign-born. Some have long beards in the style of Orthodox monastics, such as Fr. Boniface Hicks, author of *Through the Heart of St. Joseph and Fruit of Her Womb: A 33-Day Consecration to Jesus Through Mary*. Fr. Hicks is also director of spiritual formation at the seminary and has been a frequent guest on The Journey Home program on EWTN. The monastery houses over one hundred monks and is the oldest Benedictine monastery in the United States and the largest in the Western hemisphere.

Orthodox Monks

The Monastery of St. Tikhon of Zadonsk is located high in the Pocono Mountains on 300 acres of land outside Scranton, Pennsylvania, in a small town called Waymart. It was founded in 1905 by Patriarch (and Orthodox saint) Tikhon, under the auspices of the Russian Orthodox Church. Years later, the word "Russian" was dropped for the more inclusive Orthodox Church of America, or OCA. The monastery houses fourteen monks from various parts of the country.

At St. Tikhon's, the Divine Liturgy begins at 6 a.m. Participants mostly stand throughout the three-hour, incense-filled service. Chairs are available for the old and infirm, but anyone can take a seat if standing becomes unbearable. Prior to my visit, I feared that the constant standing would be less than tolerable; however, I soon found that the rhythm of the chanting and prayers produced a transcendent state that erased discomfort. After a while, I almost forgot I had legs! The sensation was a little like floating.

The contentious debate about which Church—the Roman Catholic or the Eastern Orthodox—is the true Church of the Apostles has been raging since the official split of East and West in AD 1054. Some Orthodox and Catholic clergy believe the split was a mutual parting of the ways, like a divorce, but this does not stop "experts" on both sides from wielding accusations of schism or heresy.

For Archimandrite Athanasy, a former Catholic, who lived at St. Tikhon's prior to his death in February 2016, becoming Orthodox as a young man because of the changes wrought by Vatican II merely felt like switching to a different pew in the same "universal" Church. Throughout the Orthodox world, it is a well-known fact that Fr. Athanasy fell in his childhood and was injured severely, but he prayed to, and was cured by, St. Anna, mother of the Virgin Mary. The young Athanasy then promised that when he was able and had the funds, he would order an icon of St. Anna as a prayerful "thank you."

That icon was eventually written by an Orthodox nun in 1998 in a Jerusalem convent, and in 2004 it began to stream myrrh in Fr. Athanasy's parish, All Who Sorrow, in Philadelphia, his place of residence prior to his retirement at the monastery. Many who have venerated the icon, which is now housed in a special area at St. Tikhon's, have experienced major medical cures, including from cancer. Though the icon of the Holy Righteous Anna, Mother of the Most Holy Theotokos, no longer streams myrrh, it continues to exude a sweet fragrance.

Though the young Hieromonk Sergius is St. Tikhon's abbot, the small monastery is home to several older monks with long ponytails and patriarchal beards, such as white-haired Fr. Alexander, a retired priest who could easily play Moses in an Old Testament play. He looks more like the abbot type than does the younger hieromonk. Fr. Alexander, is also a former Catholic, who joins Fr. Sergius in wearing the dramatic kamilavka hat covered with a black veil during liturgies, which helps give St. Tikhon's a "Mount Athos" look.

Most visitors to St. Tikhon's, unless traveling by car, must take a bus to Scranton (where there is no Amtrak service) and then arrange to be met by a monk who will drive them the rest of the way. My driver, the bearded Fr. Ken, met me at the station in his black cassock and black hat. In the car, he told me that before he became a monk, he spent considerable time traveling the world, and that for a time he managed restaurants in Phoenix, Arizona. Fr. Ken, who was born Orthodox and is in his early 40s, talked about entering a monastery late in life:

> It's far better to become a monastic when you are in your 20s. The problem of obedience is especially hard when you are considerably older than the abbot. Becoming a monk in your mid-20s is better, when you've had some life experiences but are still malleable or "in formation."

(Monks in the Orthodox world are called "Father" after a time of formation, though technically they might not be priests.)

After the lift from the bus station, Fr. Ken escorted me to the newly refurbished men's guesthouse. In this "off season," I was the only guest in the large bed-and-breakfast-style space, which has no television, radio, or telephones. Not far off is one of St. Tikhon's two lakes, hand-dug by the monks and stocked with fish that invariably wind up in the monastery dining room. Meals at St. Tikhon's are mostly silent affairs as monks and visitors listen to readings from the lives of the saints or the writings of the Church Fathers. In this way, it is much like a Benedictine monastery. The meal concludes when the abbot rings a handbell. Afterwards, everyone rises for a short prayer, and then, if the abbot allows it (and he almost always does), everyone resumes eating with some conversation.

Though there are many orders of Catholic monks who dress in a variety of habits, in the Orthodox world all monks dress alike: black cassock with a small, raised black hat. Orthodox monks generally do not shave or cut their hair, so depending on the monk, long hair can be bunched up in a ponytail or arranged in a "bun" of some sort to get it off the neck. The visual effects of this for the first-time visitor can be startling. One gray-haired monk's rustic appearance reminded me of the Hell's Angels, whereas a young novice, with his long hair arranged in a fan-like web at the nape of his neck, seemed to model his "look" after an angelic figure in a Byzantine icon.

Fr. Ken told me he sometimes gets mistaken for a Muslim when he goes into Scranton on monastery business. Unlike Catholic monks, who sometimes don secular clothing for trips outside the monastery, Orthodox monks wear the habit 24/7. For Fr. Ken, the hostile stares he receives caught him off guard at first, though he soon learned not to pay attention to them. "Most of the townspeople know us and enjoy seeing us," he said.

As St. Tikhon's is so small, I was able to talk with some of the monks. Although this did not always come easily for me, the process was helped considerably when Fr. Sergius announced to the group that I was visiting the monastery "to do a story for a newspaper."

Fr. Sergius, a former Catholic, went over to Orthodoxy and soon after became an Orthodox priest. The change happened, he says, because he felt that Orthodoxy offered him a life "more fully in Christ." His family "is still very much Catholic," he told me in his office in the monastery bookstore. "Ultimately, the important thing is to keep Christ as the center of our lives."

The library at St. Tikhon's contains many Catholic books, including the Catechism of the Catholic Church and books about Thomas Merton.

Br. Basil, who hails from Los Angeles, is the monastery maintenance man. He happened upon St. Tikhon's while on a job search, having worked maintenance jobs at Protestant megachurches. Exposure to the monks and the Divine Liturgy led to his conversion. As a former evangelical who was taught that drinking alcohol is always a sin, a memorable part of his conversion process was learning that Jesus did not really drink grape juice at the Last Supper but real wine, as the monks are allowed to do on Sundays, Easter, and certain feast days.

"I spent a lot of years searching," Br. Michael, the main cook, told me.

> I was an atheist, I shopped around. I'd go to Catholic and Anglican churches. Once I went into this really fancy high Anglican Church and prayed, but when communion time came around they started passing out little cups of grape juice. "No way can I do this," I thought.

Br. Michael says Orthodoxy gave him the spiritual fullness he had been searching for.

On the monastery grounds is St. Tikhon's Seminary, opened in 1937, which trains hundreds of married and unmarried men for the Orthodox priesthood. Students from the seminary sometimes work and live at the monastery for a time. Br. Jesse, a seminarian (not a monk) and also convert from evangelical Protestantism, sat near me during many noonday meals. As Orthodox priests (but not monks) can marry, Br. Jesse made several references to "finding a wife" when the time is right. Hearing seminarians talk of dating women while studying to be priests jolted my ingrained Western Catholic sensibilities.

In its 107-year history, St. Tikhon's has experienced its share of dramatic intrigue. Decades ago, a famous Serbian metropolitan was poisoned to death during an overnight visit. A man who was seen entering and leaving the metropolitan's room is suspected of poisoning the cleric. The metropolitan's vestments can be seen in St. Tikhon's museum. To illustrate the murder, an Agatha Christie-inspired tilted teacup sits on the ill-fated cleric's portable nightstand in the museum display.

Though the small number of monks at St. Tikhon's in no way matches the large number of Benedictines at St. Vincent Archabbey,

Fr. Sergius assured me there is a significant waiting list of men wishing to join, and that plans are underway to expand the monastery. Many of the monks-to-be are converts in their 20s, typical "white bread" boys from Kansas, Ohio, or Los Angeles, where they found their way—"through the grace of God," as Fr. Sergius likes to say—to this esoteric mountaintop.

My desire to visit these two monasteries came from a lifelong fascination with Catholicism and Orthodoxy. As a boy, I traveled with my family to the 1964 World's Fair in New York, where we planned to visit the Vatican pavilion. While walking there, we passed a log-cabin replica of the first Russian Orthodox church in the United States, built in California in 1825. I wanted to go inside, but it was locked. Peeking through the windows, I was startled to see a large, magnificent icon of Our Lady of Kazan in the center aisle. Later that afternoon, as my family toured the Vatican pavilion, I escaped unnoticed back to the log cabin to view the icon again.

The icon—which, as an adult, I came to see as a symbol of hope for the reunion of the two Churches—was discovered in 1579 when the Virgin Mary appeared to a Russian peasant girl and told her where to dig in the earth for an image of Our Lady. Its discovery led to miraculous cures and victory in military battles. Eventually, the image came to be known as the Protectress of Holy Russia. The icon was ushered out of the country during the Bolshevik Revolution of 1917 and wound up in Poland. For many years, the icon was in Portugal in a chapel next to the site of the 1917 apparitions of the Virgin Mary to the three children of Fatima. In 2004, Pope John Paul II returned the icon to Moscow, where today it is venerated by both Catholic and Orthodox.

The Russian Orthodox theologian Vladimir Soloviev, an intimate friend of Fyodor Dostoevsky, believed that Orthodoxy needed reunion with Rome, to whom he believed Christ gave "the keys," if it wanted to become a true universal Church rather than a dead fossil subject to the rulership of heads of state. Soloviev considered himself both Russian Orthodox and Catholic, as both Churches are truly apostolic with valid sacraments. It was Soloviev's belief that no matter who was to blame for the schism of 1054, the split led to the rise of Islam, and what followed—the fall of the Church of Constantinople—was a chastisement from God for helping to create that division. Soloviev prophesied that the salvation of the world will be found in the reunion of the two great Churches.

Two Miraculous Icons

During one of my trips to St. Tikhon's monastery, my room was very near Father Athanasay's small apartment. Father Athanasay, or so one of the monks informed me, was a former Jesuit Catholic priest who switched to Orthodoxy around the time of the Second Vatican Council. Father Athanasay's particular devotion to Saint Anna, the mother of Mary, caused him to donate a miraculous icon of Saint Anna to St. Tikhon's, although this icon did not start out as miraculous at all.

After Father Athanasay went to an iconographer to have an icon made of Saint Anna, his patron saint, the icon began to stream myrrh (perfumed oil). This fact attracted considerable attention, which inevitably led to numerous reports of miracles and healings after people prayed before the icon. The icon of Saint Anna is located in a small, separate chapel near the monastic dormitory. The chapel is large enough for fifteen monks and is sometimes used when the main church is overcrowded due to a St. Tikhon's seminary event.

A monk was kind enough to show me the icon, taking it out of its glass container so that I could get a close up view of it as well as see the gifts of jewelry, necklaces, and rings draped around the perimeter of the icon. These gifts were left by people who had benefited from miracles as a result of prayers to Saint Anna.

If you're not Catholic or Orthodox, all this might sound like hocus pocus. Some people, in fact, have suggested that the miraculous effects of the icon (or any icon) are illusionary, and that the streaming part is a hoax engineered by priests or monks just to get people to donate money or come to church. "There has to be a rational explanation," as one friend of mine insisted. I am at a loss to explain these things to skeptics, except to shrug and say that the mysteries in the universe sometimes outweigh rationality and logic. Sometimes there is no rational explanation. When the monk first showed me the icon of Saint Anna, I didn't smell perfume or see it stream myrrh, but I did cross myself and give it a kiss.

Two days later, I would visit Saint George's Orthodox Greek Catholic church in Taylor, Pennsylvania, when the abbot of St. Tikhon's invited me to accompany one of the monks and his visiting parents to a service around the exposition of two weeping icons that had been attracting considerable attention.

For at least two years these icons of the Virgin Mary (Theotokos) have exuded a fragrant oil or perfume-like substance that literally flows down the surface of the icon, so much so that it can be collected in a bottle or swabbed up with cotton balls. Sometimes the streaming is so intense it fogs the outer glass containers into which the icons are placed. The service, called a Moleben, is about forty minutes of prayers and hymns, during which the priest places the icons on a Tetrapod (or stand) and then anoints the congregants with the myrrh. In the past, the Moleben has attracted thousands of people, some of whom have reported healings of serious back pain and stroke-related problems. I was told that there were so many people at the service one year that the local police had to direct traffic in and out of the church parking lot.

The people who attend these services are Orthodox, Roman, and Byzantine Catholic Christians. In the Catholic world, there are statues and pictures of the Virgin Mary that also weep. But this is not about seeing the face of Jesus or Mary in a grilled cheese sandwich or the swirl of a Dairy Crème ice cream cone. The media favors these frivolous stories because they tend to poke fun at crazy religious people duped by superstition. There is nothing laughable about an icon that weeps.

That is why when the abbot, Father Sergius, asked me if I would like to accompany a young monk and his parents to see these icons, I replied with curious enthusiasm. On the evening of the service, I met up with Father Silouan, the young bearded monk who converted to Orthodoxy several years ago after finding himself in a rut while attending art school.

Father Silouan, who was at that time an iconographer at St. Tikhon's, changed his mind about a career as a secular artist when the instructors at the art school he was attending announced they would begin to teach students how to sell and make money from their art. The future monk, cooled by this emphasis on money, announced that he was not interested in doing art for cash. As a result, he left art school and then, through a serendipitous chain of events, happened to find himself inside an Orthodox church after one of his friends told him that he "should take a look at this place."

Father Silouan took to Orthodoxy like a fish to water, and not long after entered the monastery at St. Tikhon's. But for his parents it was a slightly longer road. While traveling with Father Silouan's family, his mother told me that she was at first a little put off by her son's conversion. For many Protestant evangelicals, like Father Silouan's mom, Orthodoxy can seem like voodoo with its icons, candles, incense, and blatantly un-modern vestments. Nevertheless, both she and her husband followed their son's path. For Fr. Silouan's father, who was born Catholic, the transition was easier. He told me that following his son was like going back to the Church of his childhood before Vatican II.

Fr. Silouan's mother recalled the initial reactions of her evangelical friends when she told them she was now Orthodox: "It's superstition, almost witchcraft!" some of them replied. Of course, her friends were thinking about the icons, and how they saw them as idol worship, even if they did not realize that prayers are said to the saint the icon represents, not to the icon *per se* (as an idol). Icons, simply put, are not worshipped. Catholics get similar criticisms when some insist that they pray to statues, not to the saint a statue represents. Father Silouan's mother found explaining these things to her questioning friends to be a hopelessly frustrating experience.

"This is the original Christianity," she told me she informed them. "Before there was scripture—before there was a Bible—there was liturgy."

The church was crowded when we arrived. There were Greeks, non-Greeks, non-Christians, workmen who looked as though they had just left a construction site, elderly couples, and people with obvious medical conditions, families, children, and curiosity-seekers. The two icons, in glass containers, were placed front and center before the iconostasis. The priest, in blue vestments, chanted a prayer that elicited robust responses from the hundreds present. The energy in that small church had an upward drift, even a touch of the charismatic—but just a touch, because the Orthodox never go overboard with these things. You will not find hand-waving, head rolling, or snake charming.

By the time we made our way to the icons to get anointed from the streaming myrrh, the entire church had the smell of roses. We watched as the priest would switch from one icon to another, sometimes holding one aloft but at an angled position so that the myrrh would run in a steady stream into the cupped hands of congregants. The streams of myrrh were constant. When it was my turn, my forehead was swabbed with the fragrant oil. Some people were in tears.

For a good ten minutes or so in the car on the way back to the monastery, nobody said a word. We were all still in the perfumed environment of the church.

The tempo changed when Fr. Silouan announced that, compliments of the abbot, we would be stopping at a Chinese restaurant for a bite to eat because we had missed dinner at the monastery.

We continued to talk about what we had experienced through dinner, feeling very good that we had witnessed a true … miracle.

Orthodox royals

Little children under the age of seven will take to trembling and die in the arms of the people who hold them; others will do penance through hunger … The seasons will have changed.

—Our Lady of La Salette

When the Princess of Battenberg and Grand Duchess Elizabeth converted to Orthodox Christianity, there was a negative reaction among their royal relatives. Orthodoxy was viewed as exotic, with its veneration of icons and long, elaborate services, a sort of "foreign import Church" that in some ways put the two women converts at an odd angle to their former lives as western Christians.

Queen Victoria, for instance, was not pleased when the Grand Duchess began venerating icons and expressed an interest in Orthodoxy.

Both women came from Protestant backgrounds, as did Nicholas II's wife, Alexandra, who was German and born a Lutheran. Princess Ileana of Romania, though not an Orthodox convert, had always secretly entertained thoughts of entering monastic life, despite her two marriages, the first to Archduke Anton of Austria in 1931—the couple had six children— the second to Dr. Stefan Nicolaus Issarescu in June 1954, one month after her official divorce from Anton. Issarescu and Ileana were later divorced, and in 1961 Ileana entered a French monastery, where she eventually took vows as a nun, becoming Mother Alexandra.

Having fled Romania in 1948 with her family—she was given a choice by the provisional communist government to flee the country or be executed—she first went to Switzerland and then Argentina, but in 1950 she traveled to the United States for medical treatment, where she also planned to establish a home for herself and her family outside Boston. The story of how she managed her affairs after a life in the royal courts of Europe, and how she came to the conclusion that she was always meant to be a monastic, will be explored in this book.

The communist coup in Romania in 1944 was the result of years of internal struggles between pro-German alliances, the Romanian monarchy—as represented by Queen Marie, the mother of Princess Ileana and King Carol II, Ileana's older brother—as well as a number of smaller revolutionary factions attempting to tighten their grip on the reins of government. The mid-1940s was a watershed period, when the infiltrating communists were suddenly everywhere.

Father Roman Braga, a priest, monk, and theologian—and now up for sainthood in the Romanian Orthodox Church— was thrown into prison in the mid-1950s when the Romanian communist government made a serious attempt at suppressing monastic life. In his book, *Journey to Simplicity—The Life and Wisdom of Archimandrite Roman Braga*, author Daniel B. Hinshaw tells Fr. Braga's story in great detail, describing how the communists undermined the foundations of Romanian society before implementing their "atheistic utopian for Romania."

As Braga observes:

Suddenly we found ourselves in the presence of Communism, this beast with an apocalyptic stench, with an odor of vodka and military sweat, filling the whole country with posters announcing carnivals and meetings; it was a time of yellow press, political prostitution, and a reversal of values. We were overwhelmed with the fear that

these waves of evil would transform us all into an anonymous mass
without form, without conscience, without responsibility.

Romania, as part of the larger vanquished Soviet family of states
created by the Russian Revolution of 1918, underwent the same
sort of indoctrination that Russian citizens endured after the
dethronement of the monarchy. Cynical party apparatchiks, writes
Hinshaw, knew they had to address a fundamental problem
confronting and potentially confounding any plan for pacifying
and indoctrinating the new satellite nations added to the Soviet
orbit. Clearly, small children would be amenable over time to
indoctrination in communist theories and doctrines as they grew
up in a new educational system purged of petty bourgeois and
religious thought.

Decades of this sort of reeducation and brainwashing still retain
their power, even after the liberalizing revolutions that followed.
A case illustrative of this is the feminist punk band Pussy Riot
controversy in Moscow long after the fall of the Iron Curtain
in 1991.

An orthodox monastery conversion story

> If ever I had a regret, it is that I could not have become a monk—an
> idea which kept occurring to me in the cauchemar of Sotheby's.
> I'd explain to you one day why I could never join the Catholic
> Church, since I believe that the churches of the Eastern Rite are the
> True Church. I have recently learned that there is no contradiction
> between the Anglican and Orthodox. God willing, it seems possible
> that I could become a lay brother.
>
> —Bruce Chatwin

While reading Salman Rushdie's *Joseph Anton*, the story of
Rushdie's life in hiding after he was sentenced to death by the
Ayatollah Khomeini on February 14, 1989, I came across a
reference to English writer Bruce Chatwin.

Born in 1940, Chatwin, an English novelist and travel writer, was
one of the most prominent people in Britain to die of HIV-AIDS in
1989. As a young man, Chatwin worked at Sotheby's in London

until he contracted an eye problem, at which point his interests began to turn towards archeology. Although gay, he married Elizabeth Chanler, a descendent of John Jacob Astor, in 1965. Their marriage was celibate, according to Chatwin's biographer, Nicholas Alexander.

Chatwin, in fact, was never open about his homosexuality or about his contracting HIV-AIDS, a disease he kept secret or passed off as a fungal infection caused by a monkey bite during one of his travels. He also claimed that he contracted the disease from a gang rape or a possible transmission from Sam Wagstaff, photographer Robert Mapplethorpe's lover.

A 2017 article in *The Guardian* noted that it was in 1982, while leafing through *Time* magazine, that Chatwin came across an article about a "gay plague":

> He later told his wife, Elizabeth, that he had immediately thought this applied to him. In his final years, sometimes feverish, sometimes high on the drugs he was prescribed, he became an exaggerated version of his already high-velocity self. He was full of plans and wheezes. He wanted to write a mighty novel featuring "four decadent countries—the USA, the USSR, France and Britain."

To most people, Chatwin was a good-looking blond Nordic type with a slender frame. It is said that when he walked into a room, all eyes—male and female—turned to him. Here was not only beauty, but substance and brains. Chatwin's looks, however, did not impress novelist Christopher Isherwood. In his diaries, Isherwood notes (on September 28, 1972):

> Yesterday we had a visit from Bruce Chatwin, a blond, blue-eyed but somehow not really attractive friend of Peter Schlesinger. He is an anthropologist—and has spent time with native groups of hunters in the lands south of the Sahara; Mali, Niger and Chad. He was extremely interesting, describing how the boys between thirteen and sixteen wear a sort of drag and are regarded as girls.

Chatwin spent the winter of 1979 in New York City, where he mingled with Robert Mapplethorpe, art historian John Richardson, novelist Edmund White and Jacqueline Onassis. In a letter to Elizabeth, his wife, he wrote:

> Life in New York highly social. Dinner parties every night. Escorting Mrs. Onassis to the opera next Thursday. Met her again with the John Russells, and my God she's fly. Far more subtle than any American woman I've ever met.

Chatwin wrote that Mrs. Onassis's whisper was conspiratorial, not affected: "The whisper of a naughty child egging you on to do something mildly wicked. To behave badly without being rude."

"The most beautiful Cezanne in the world is to my mind Henry McIllhenny's Portrait of Madame Cezanne," Chatwin wrote to a friend when describing a visit to McIllhenny's townhouse on Philadelphia's Rittenhouse Square. "He is a nice, tough, open-minded man, who likes Australia a lot, and has of course recently sold the wonderful, but very conventional still-life to pay for his yacht."

The author of nine books, including *Patagonia* (1977) and *On the Black Hill* (1982), Chatwin called himself a nomad, writing that a nomad never has to worry about finding God or the finality of death, because the act of moving wards off all such concerns.

One critic observed that "Chatwin's … big idea was that nomadism is the true condition of man, that natural selection has fitted the human race for wandering, not for a sedentary life, and that the ills of civilization issue from the neglect of this nomadic imperative."

As a writer, Chatwin rarely mentioned God or played up any interest in spirituality. Indeed, he is often remembered for the following quote: "I haven't got any special religion this morning. My God is the God of Walkers. If you walk hard enough, you probably don't need any other god."

But when he traveled to Mount Athos to visit a monastery and observe the daily lives of Orthodox monks, Chatwin was struck by a large iron cross in the rocks overlooking the sea. When he saw the cross, he stopped dead in his tracks. He knew instantly that his nomadic (non-spiritual) days were over. He soon made plans to convert to the Orthodox Christian faith, and wanted Metropolitan Kallistos Ware, a convert to Orthodoxy from Anglicanism, to baptize him. Death intervened before that could happen, but Chatwin was given an Orthodox funeral at Saint Sophia Church in London, attended by Salman Rushdie and a number of writers from the United States and Britain.

Rushdie, in a similar satirical tone to that in *The Satanic Verses* which landed him in hot water with the Ayatollah, described Chatwin's funeral liturgy as follows:

> Its rituals were ornately Byzantine. Blah blah blah Bruce Chatwin, intoned the priests, blah blah Chatwin blah blah. They stood up, they sat down, they knelt, they stood and then sat again. The air was full of the stink of holy smoke.

Rushdie called the liturgy Chatwin's last great joke.

But it was hardly a joke. While staying at the Serbian monastery of Chilandari on Mount Athos, Chatwin would wake up at 5:30 every morning to attend services. One afternoon, while visiting the monastery of Stavronikita (once painted by Edward Lear), he encountered an iron cross on a rock that inspired him to write, "There must be a God."

Susannah Clapp, one of Chatwin's editors, wrote that the writer's funeral was "a mysterious event, unlike any other memorial service I have ever attended." She went on to explain that while many thought it beautiful, "others thought its theatricality camp." Writer Martin Amis, like Rushdie, noted that the funeral service was "Bruce's last joke on his friends and loved ones."

Rushdie, who as a boy was taken by his father to a mosque where there was "a good deal of up-down forehead bumping, and standing up with your palms held in front of you like a book, and much mumbling of unknown words in a language I didn't speak," comes from a place where religion is antithetical to the life of the mind. Call it the Ayn Rand school of Disembodied Theology, the "I only believe in me" world that many intelligent people inhabit.

Intellectuals like Rushdie, then, become nervous when their peers "find religion" or alter old agnostic courses for new "believing" ones. They either react with bemused tolerance, skepticism ("It has to be a joke"), or outright hostility, as Virginia Woolf did upon hearing of T. S. Eliot's conversion to Anglo-Catholicism.

Woolf was not amused at her friend's transition, but in fact became very angry. She even predicted that Eliot would "drop his Christianity with his wife, as one might empty the fishbones after the herring." But that is not what happened at all.

Pussy Riot and sacred spaces

When the sassy members of Pussy Riot entered Moscow's Christ the Savior Cathedral in February 2012, it was not to pray or to sit in silent meditation, but to stage a sanctuary protest before the iconostasis and Royal Doors, also known as the Beautiful Gate that leads to the altar area.

In various YouTube videos of the protest, one can see the women bowing and crossing themselves in the manner of ardent believers. The songs the women sing have radically different lyrics than the sung prayers that usually come from this space, and yet one clearly gets the impression that the feminist band members grew up in the Orthodox faith. In fact, there is nothing satirical in the way the women cross themselves; they do so in the fervent style of old women in head scarves. The "prayer" they say also tells a different story: it was a plea to the Lord to oust Russian President Vladimir Putin.

While Pussy Riot did not destroy or endanger church property— there was no splattered paint, no drawn graffiti, no bombs, hand grenade explosions, or tarnished icons—the crude punk protest song delivered in the style of a prayer hit a chord with many Russians. The scene brought to mind the far more radical actions of ACT UP in December 1989, when several dozen members of the group went into New York's Saint Patrick's Cathedral and disrupted Mass with shouts of "We will not be silent" to protest the New York Archdiocese's views on AIDS and abortion. One protestor even desecrated the Eucharist as others scattered condoms about the church.

Had Pussy Riot "acted up" in a New York City church, it is highly likely they would not have been arrested. Furthermore, Pussy Riot's actions would probably not have even made the local news. To American eyes and ears, the Kremlin's reaction to the crude protest was extreme, almost as if the punk band had been involved in a plot to kill Vladimir Putin. "It was just a song, after all," many said.

When Pussy Riot members Maria Alyokhina and Nadezhda Tolokonnikova were given prison sentences of two years for "hooliganism with religious hatred," there was considerable international protest. Many saw the punishment as outstripping the crime.

In a surprise protest, a 75-year-old Orthodox priest, the Rev. Pavel Adelglim, stated publicly that the severe sentence underscored the Russian Orthodox Church's close ties with the Kremlin. Adelglim wrote on his blog: "The women have unmasked the lie of the Russian Orthodox Church and its unnatural bond with the Russian Federation."

In October, 2013, it was reported that Tolokonnikova, who had been sentenced to the Gulag-style prison in Mordovia, was quietly removed to an undisclosed penal colony. This reportedly upset her husband, who claimed that the authorities were trying to stop the publicity surrounding his wife's prison hunger strike. Tolokonnikova herself had claimed that she had been abused by Mordovia prison guards since the first day of her imprisonment. Both Alyokhina and Tolokonnikova were released in 2013.

A fortunate third Pussy Riot member, Katarina Samutsevich, was released earlier in a special arrangement with prosecutors.

Eager to understand the situation, I arranged to speak with Father Mark Shinn, archpriest and pastor of Saint Andrew's (Russian) Orthodox Cathedral in Philadelphia. As an Orthodox Christian, it was important for me to make sense of the lengthy prison sentences for what appeared to be a rude but nevertheless benign protest. In the United States, people receive two-year prison sentences for second degree manslaughter, major thefts, random felonies, or domestic abuse, not for so-called blasphemous acts. To the modern mind, a blasphemous act is often associated with perceived religious offenses in Islamic countries.

At some point before my visit to Father Shinn, it occurred to me what would have happened if Pussy Riot had performed their crude act in Saint Peter's in Rome immediately after the election of Pope Francis. Given the unpredictable nature of the new pope, it is quite conceivable that, in the spirit of humility and reconciliation, he would have insisted the band be pardoned, and then invited the women to tea or a round of vodka toasting in his Vatican office. While hundreds of Russian petitioners did send their plea to the Orthodox patriarch for a pardon, no olive branch was extended.

Arriving at Saint Andrew's, Father Shinn, who converted to Orthodoxy as a teenager, offered me a seat in the church hall. After a round of polite pleasantries, we quickly segued into Pussy Riot and the notion of what constitutes a sacred space. To that end, he reminded me that in the American colonial era, the first churches—namely the Congregational churches (or descendants of the Puritans) —thought of the church building as having a dual purpose: they were meeting places as well as places of prayer. The Congregational idea of a dual-purpose church building quickly filtered down into most Protestant denominations.

Father Shinn explained:

Leafing through old Congregational handbooks and manuals it is clear that these churches were constructed as meeting and prayer houses. This becomes clear when you watch reruns of *Little House on the Prairie,* where the church and school house are one and the same thing. In the nineteenth century and earlier, traveling magistrates held court in these combination prayer/meeting houses. There was absolutely no sense of these meeting houses as a sacred space dedicated solely to the worship of God. That has been the reality for American Protestant churches for generations. The idea of a sacred space devoted solely to the worship of God did not exist.

Of course, one has only to consider how the average Hollywood film confuses the notion of what constitutes a sacred space. Very often, when Christian religious services are pictured in movies, there are glaring mismatches: a large Bible on an altar while the presiding (Protestant) minister makes the sign of the cross or uses holy water. Or a Protestant minister preaching to a congregation before a statue of the Virgin Mary. Sometimes Hollywood will even call a Protestant service a Mass, or have a decidedly southern Baptist congregation genuflect before entering a pew. These hybrid Hollywood movie religious services contain so many Catholic and Protestant cross-elements it is clear that nobody knows what they are doing. Illustrating further,

Father Shinn mentions a Robert Redford film, *The Bear Field War*, where the filmmakers had a community meeting take place in a Catholic church, but before the meeting begins a woman gets up and lights a candle as if it is the beginning of a religious service.

In both Orthodoxy and Catholicism, a church is considered a temple of God, not a place for the traveling magistrate, a puppet show, a rock band, or groups of money changers. In ancient Judaism, the temple (or sacred space) had an inner court where sacrifices and cleansings were offered. There were also a series of curtains where only priests could go to offer prayers and incense, then the Holy of Holies, divided by yet another curtain (and corresponding to the average Orthodox church), where the Arks of the Covenant lay and where only the High Priest could pass.

Unfortunately, since the close of the Second Vatican Council, many modern Catholic churches reflect conventional Spartan Protestant church interiors. In some cases the interiors of these churches are devoid of sacred images and iconography, so their identification as "Catholic" seems remote at best. Many of these churches have become, at least by default, Congregational-style meeting places.

The special history of Moscow's Christ the Savior Cathedral must also be understood when gauging the anger of the average Russian at Pussy Riot's antics.

The idea to build the original cathedral came from Emperor Alexander I, who wanted to commemorate Napoleon's retreat from Moscow. Father Shinn explained:

> Napoleon entered Russia with 485,000 men on Christmas Day, 1812, but when he left the country he left with 43,000 men. Less than 10 percent survived the invasion. During that time, the French desecrated Russia's churches. They used Russian church sanctuaries as stables; they had parties with prostitutes on altars.

To celebrate Napoleon's retreat, the first cathedral was built by donations from the people. The state offered no support. The composer Tchaikovsky even got into the act and planned to perform his *1812 Overture* when the church was completed. Work on the first church was halted due to problems with the design, which included an emphasis on neoclassicism and Freemasonic symbols. Originally constructed on Sparrow Hill, the highest point in Moscow, Alexander's successor, Nicholas I, especially objected to the Freemasonic symbols and employed a new architect, Konstantin Thon. After the new design, construction commenced. By the time the scaffolding was removed in 1860, and the church was consecrated in 1883, it was known as the tallest Orthodox church in the world, at 338 feet.

Although the church survived the beginnings of the Russian Revolution, on December 5, 1931, on orders from Joseph Stalin, it was slated for demolition, but first it would be robbed of all valuable artifacts—icons, vestments, chalices, and the 20 tons of gold on the domes that authorities deemed to be of "excellent quality." It took two dynamite blasts to demolish the church and at least a year to completely clear the site of debris. The plan was to replace the cathedral with a huge tower, the Palace of the Soviets, which would be topped off with a statue of Lenin, but flooding problems from the nearby Moskva River and a lack of funds prevented completion of the memorial. Nikita Khrushchev would later open a public swimming pool on the site.

Father Shinn added:

> When the Soviet Union fell, it was agreed that Russia would rebuild the church. The old Soviet economy had collapsed, replaced by robber barons, yet with the tenacity of the Jewish mayor of Moscow, work on the new building went on twenty-four hours a day, with shifts around the clock and the use of spotlights. The result was a better church, a symbol of the rebirth of the Church after seventy years of atheism and the Revolution.

One can almost say that the cathedral was built with blood, sweat, and tears, and that its reopening after the deadly years of communism was nothing less than a miracle. Nobody expected to see communism fall in the twentieth century, or even witness the rebirth of the Orthodox Church in Russia.

While Father Shinn can hardly be summed up as a heartless hardliner, during our conversation he wanted me to understand that almost everybody in Russia—he emphasized the word "everybody"— was horrified at Pussy Riot's disrespectful act in such a symbolic place.

Even to people who were not churchgoers even for these people the disrespect showed by Pussy Riot brought back horrible memories. Non-believers, or atheists, were also horrified. They understood almost "genetically" that this is something not acceptable. You do not desecrate holy places.

Russian non-believers and even atheists were horrified at the punk band's protest. Is this classified information? I wondered why this fact did not make it to the copy room of *The New York Times* and the nation's wire services.

Shortly after Pussy Riot's cathedral stunt, a new law was instituted making it a criminal offense to offend the religious sensitivities of any Russian religion.

"The penalties became more severe if the desecration takes place within as opposed to without," Father Shinn said, adding that the two cultures—American and Russian—just do not understand one another. "Americans do not understand the reverence for sacred places, while Russians cannot understand the American callousness towards houses of worship."

As if to prove this point, not long after my conversation with Fr. Shinn, I researched a Sacred Space II seminar in Pasadena, California, where representatives from many Protestant denominations and liberal Jewish synagogues discussed the idea of sacred spaces. Among the many matters discussed during the conference were questions like "do you want your sacred space to feel like a home, or do you want it to be transcendent?"

Dr. William Dyrness, a professor of theology and culture at Fuller Theological School, summed up his response at the conference as follows: "Protestantism doesn't include a belief in sacred space, because all space is sacred."

So, there we have it. If all spaces are sacred, then Pussy Riot did nothing wrong; but if some places are more sacred than others, then we might be said to have a real problem.

Displaced royalty

I have included the following sections regarding Prince Harry and his Hollywood wife, Meghan Markle, because I felt they related to the complex, secretive, and Machiavellian discord common in many royal families. This really became apparent to me when I interviewed Dominic Habsburg, Ileana's sole surviving son, about his own royal experiences. Furthermore, although they come from different royal families, Harry, like Ileana, was also related to Queen Victoria, who was his great-great-great-grandmother.

The British Royal Family and the unconventional antics of Prince Harry and Meghan Markle led me to an astounding book, *Meghan and Harry, The Real Story*. The author, Lady Colin Campbell, is *The New York Times* bestselling author of biographies of Princess Diana, the Queen Mother, and Queen Elizabeth II.

Lady C, as she is called, hails from a wealthy Jamaican family (Ziadie). She grew up in the United States and met her former husband, Lord Colin Campbell—the brother of the twelfth Duke of Argyll—in 1974. Their marriage lasted just fourteen months. In 2013, she bought Castle Goring in West Sussex, England, at that point a complete ruin with crumbling walls and one functioning bathroom. To finance the cost of a new roof, Lady C appeared as a contestant in Britain's popular reality TV show *I'm a Celebrity ... Get Me Out of Here!*

I interviewed Lady C on Zoom from her Castle Goring home.

Castle Goring was designed by John Rebecca for Sir Bysshe Shelley, the grandfather of the poet, Percy Bysshe Shelley. Shelley's death at age 29 prevented him from living in the castle, although it was his wife Mary Shelley's home for a time.

Lady C's book is a virtual X-ray of Harry and Meghan, who in 2020 opted to trade their royal status for a life of Hollywood visibility.

Lady C is quick to say that Meghan is far more intelligent and worldly-wise than Harry, "who has spent his whole life being cosseted by nannies, servants, private detectives, staff and courtiers."

When I ask whether the couple stepped out on Sunday to attend church, Lady C replies:

> I think Harry worships at the altar of Meghan, and she worships at the altar of celebrity. Meghan has been Catholic, Jewish, and Church of England, so you could say she has something going on with the world of religion. I think they ultimately believe that God should serve them as opposed to them serving God.

In the book, Lady C quotes an astrologer who predicted a long and fruitful marriage for the pair. This contrasts with a number of You Tube psychics (the list is exhaustive) who have forecast a breakup once Meghan has had her fill of Harry and established herself as "The Most Famous Woman in the World" (something she is committed to doing since signing on with public relations firm Sunshine Sachs).

Lady C believes their marriage is very strong, despite the predictions of those who wish to see the union fail. "I actually think their marriage is a lot stronger than their detractors say it is." Those detractors often base their claim on the fact that Harry looks miserable in pictures. "But Harry has always been miserable. He's a spoiled brat," Lady C says.

The American public generally view Harry and Meghan in a more favorable light than do the British, seeing them as being on a quest for independence from an outdated monarchy that no longer has any relevance. Yet any astute observer can see that since his marriage to Meghan, Harry is no longer as much fun as he was before they met. "Now he has to save the world for her. Woke rhetoric, hyper-political attitudinizing, yoga and meditation have replaced the fun sessions the couple had enjoyed prior to meeting each other," Lady C writes. She continues:

> Since their marriage, the couple has been pushing the boundaries. They have been breeching rules, protocols, and agreements with a degree of alacrity which is actually frightening. This is happening on the basis of "Let's see what we can get away with while things are still up in the air."

The Queen, who died in 2022, gave the couple one year to try out their "half in and half out" hybrid lifestyle, but once the trial period ended, Buckingham Palace planned to weigh in on what was to be. Lady C predicted that Harry and Meghan were never going to wait for the Queen's royal edict, but had already been "discussing the voluntary release of their titles so that she [Meghan] can muck in the political which as royals they are not allowed to do."

This is precisely what happened. The couple disengaged from the royal family and moved to California in June 2020, stating they wanted space to raise their son, Archie. A daughter, Lilibet, was born in California in 2021. The couple no longer has an official UK residence. In 2023, they were asked by his father, King Charles III, to vacate Frogmore Cottage, a house on the Windsor estate.

"The British monarchy is not a television show," Lady C says, leaning forward into the Zoom camera for special emphasis. "It's one of the most eminent institutions in the world and I think it is almost laughable that Meghan has this almost complete disdain for the royal family and the institution of the monarchy."

She adds that Meghan has modeled herself on Princess Diana, a maverick and rebel,

> who until the end of her life was trying to position herself to try to be bigger than the royal family. Diana was cleverer than Meghan. Meghan is flagrant, Diana was obtuse. Diana understood that she was not in such a position of power; Meghan actually thinks she's a great power broker.

At the time of the couple's wedding, Meghan's father, Thomas Markle, was generally portrayed in the United States as a publicity-seeking buffoon, but according to Lady C that is the opposite of the truth. Her book lays out all of Meghan's lies and obfuscations about her father. Lady C wrote that Meghan's pretensions about being a new sort of "peoples' princess" fall apart when one considers how deeply ashamed she is of her birth family.

> Everything Meghan said about her father 2 weeks before she met Harry contradicted the assertions that were being made on Meghan's behalf through Harry. I was outraged, and I will go to my grave outraged. It was one of the lowest things that any human being can do to another human being. To do it to a parent showed me the nature of what we're dealing with. It chilled my blood. I have a great deal of sympathy for Thomas Markle. I also know how completely devastated he has been by the loss of the daughter that he thought he had. It's almost like a Greek tragedy, it's that profound.

The British monarchy welcomed Meghan into their ranks as a woman of color, not that Meghan looked like a person of color at all. Lady C continues:

Meghan and Harry have both played the color card not only in terms of the British nation but in terms of the Royal Family. So the Royal Family has had to be very careful to be seen bending over backwards to be seen to be accommodating ... also the Royal Family understands that Harry is a very disturbed individual.

The Crown welcomed Meghan with open arms, but she returned that welcome by treating her staff in impolite ways. Shortly after her marriage, Lady C says, Meghan hurled a dress onto the floor "that had not been ironed to her exacting standards." In yet another incident with staff, she continues, Meghan "lost her temper and threw a hot beverage in the direction of someone who had annoyed her. This had resulted in the member of the staff resigning and being paid £250,000 to leave without disclosing the incident."
Meghan, Lady C says, is ruthlessly ambitious:

She was a second-rate Hollywood actress who didn't even have a career in Hollywood. She's an arriviste who doesn't have the character, the demeanor, the modesty to understand that she was given one of the greatest roles on earth.

Lady C has the sort of infectious laugh that makes you curious as to what she will say next. She tells me about the time she almost knocked the Queen over when the Queen opened the door in her flat, thinking she was doing Lady C a favor by letting her dogs out. "She was really a great gal, as you Americans would say."
What about Harry, the disturbed individual?

There was an incident many years ago when Harry at a private event tried to physically attack a friend of mine for no reason at all. Harry is also very paranoid. He's a puffed-up character who complains about everything, a person full of his own importance. Harry also suffers from rage. He is the typical spoiled brat second son. You guys in America don't really understand the whole business of being the second son.

Lady C provides me with some "facts" about Harry:
He was desperate to get married but none of the well-bred girls wanted to marry him.

Meghan, when she realized that Harry was a marriage possibility, read up on Diana's life and copied everything Diana did, including wearing the same perfume.

When Meghan became pregnant with Archie—the name "Archie" was also an insult, since "Archie"' is a name royals usually call their dogs—she clutched her pregnancy bump whenever she could while wearing tight clothing. That was never done before. She was behaving like trailer trash. It appalled all segments of the British population.

Meghan wants to be the most famous human being on earth. But you cannot be hyper-famous unless you are controversial, unless your reputation is a mixed bag.

So Meghan jumps on the bandwagon with the Obamas and by inviting Hilary Clinton to tea at Frogmore Cottage and then leaking that news to the newspapers, while she does not go to a state event at Buckingham Palace because she doesn't approve of Donald Trump—all of this is deeply disturbing but it gets her the attention she wants.

Meghan cares about Hollywood, the Bill Gateses, the Obamas and the Clintons of this world. She has calculated that they are her meal ticket to billionaire status and possibly political power.

The second son

Prince Harry used to be thought of as the jolly good royal, a "game" guy who never let his quest for adventure get in the way of family loyalty. The ginger prince had no fear about leaving the palace and engaging in edgy military endeavors, even if he occasionally slipped into "bad boy" behavior.

The UK public easily forgave him these improprieties, never forgetting that he was left motherless as a young boy and that his bad behavior was likely due to emotional scars.

While many then might have questioned Prince Harry's maturity, there was never a question about his sanity—until he met Meghan Markle, an obscure Hollywood actress who at some point in her career had sold her soul to woke forces and then set about transforming Harry into a puppet to do her political bidding.

Today, Prince Harry is a very different kind of "bad boy." He is on a mission to save the world, and that has caused the once happy grandson of Queen Elizabeth to believe he is some kind of Messiah.

Pride and narcissism often comes with a Messiah complex, as does a personality change. In Harry's case, he has become unhappy and grumpy as his woke wife pushes him further and further into political black holes.

Markle, of course, has made no secret of her desire to be the most famous woman in the world. To meet this goal, she has even employed a public relations agency, Hollywood's Sunshine Sachs, to make sure she is constantly in the public eye.

"Positive publicity never gives sufficient column-inches to fame-hungry people. The only thing that keeps the flame of fame flickering brightly is variability. The narrative has to have twists and turns, negativity and positivity," Lady Colin Campbell wrote of Markle's quest for fame in her book, *Meghan and Harry, The Real Story.*

It is obvious that the change in Prince Harry since his marriage can no longer be laughed off as if it was a Bill Maher joke on woke inanities.

Indeed, the time has come for the royal family to immediately apply the full brakes on Harry by eliminating all of his titles and categorizing him as a "former royal." The time for indecision and waiting is over, as evidenced by Harry's 2022 address at the United Nations on Nelson Mandela International Day.

What the former prince has become was in full display in that nearly empty UN room as he began to pontificate, albeit in a rather clunky way, his views on climate change, the 2020 pandemic, the Ukraine war, and—what was most unsettling to him—the U.S. Supreme Court's overturning of Roe vs Wade, which he termed a grave threat to democracy and a misreading of the Constitution.

In that UN speech, Harry broke a cardinal rule for royals that they must never comment publicly on geopolitical decisions. Then again, Harry wants to exist in both worlds, the royal one (when he desires a speaking platform) and the non-royal world, when he wants to be a Californian while working as an activist revolutionary to align the world with the new agenda we see being promoted

24/7 in the legacy media, pre-kindergarten classrooms, universities, corporations, and even in local neighborhood associations.

You cannot serve two masters, however, without cutting off the arms and legs of one, which in Harry's case means the British Royal Family is on the chopping block.

He made his choice clearly known during his twenty-minute UN speech in which he mentioned "weaponising lies and disinformation at the expense of the man," a vague left-wing cult phrase that dubs any fact or narrative outside the woke narrative as false.

When he referenced "Africa being mired in poverty"—a phrase that anyone can say to prove any point whatsoever—he showed a schoolboy intellectual shallowness, as if Africa being mired in poverty was somehow the world's fault and that solutions could be found if only we—with the UN's help—work to "end poverty."

I am reminded of an eighth-grade teacher reading essay submissions from students in which a quarter of the class says that their goal for the world is "to end poverty."

Since his UN speech was Nelson Mandela International Day, it was his "duty" to mention Africa, in conjunction with the photograph he was referencing of his mother, Princess Diana, posing with Mandela, a special gift to him by none other than Archbishop Desmond Tutu.

This icon was the Holy Grail, his blessing from heaven to continue where he thinks his mother left off in her various short (and at times justified) social justice crusades before her death.

The Spectator aptly noted that the zeitgeist of Harry's speech had its roots in the fact that the speaker was "clothed in the enduring righteousness of Mandela," which gave it "an importance that, based on its contents, it once again doesn't deserve."

Especially galling was hearing the prince expound on diminishing freedoms in the United States because of the Supreme Court's Roe v Wade decision, while completely ignoring any mention of the UK's draconian laws on free speech, where one can be imprisoned or questioned by the police for seeming to say something that might be interpreted by someone as possibly inciting feelings of hate or discrimination.

In 2019, the crackdown on free speech throughout the UK was so widespread that the head of the National Police Chiefs' Council warned the focus on investigating hate crimes was putting a strain on police resources at a time when the country was dealing with rising levels of violence.

And yet here was Harry, his hair thicker and curlier than it appeared in former photos, his beard a lot scruffier, while he also seemed to be sporting a significant weight gain—the privileged life of an activist ex-royal—pretending to know more about the U.S. Constitution than the average citizen of that country.

Markle has destroyed the unity in her own family by perpetuating schisms among relatives and then walking away without attempting any sort of reconciliation or redemption. The ex-Hollywood actress apparently cannot help herself as she chips away at the unity of the royal family via manipulations of Harry, while her own family smolders in ruins.

To that end, she has continued to ignore pleas for reconciliation from her father, Thomas, who lives alone in Mexico. She has also ignored her sister, Samantha, who once said of Markle: "She broke up one family; she'll break up the Royal family."

1

The Last Romanian Princess

I am on Amtrak's *The Pennsylvanian*, traveling from Philadelphia to Pittsburgh to visit the last Romanian princess.

Not the princess in person, of course, but an important part of her legacy. Arranging this trip seemed as difficult as planning a journey to Romania. Figuring out how to get to Ellwood City, Pennsylvania, from the City of Steel presented a host of problems. Ellwood City is where the princess—in her new incarnation as Mother Alexandra—founded the Orthodox Monastery of the Transfiguration in 1965. The most efficient ways to get there are by taxi or Uber. There are shuttle buses that go to Ellwood, but they mostly operate during the day. *The Pennsylvanian* was due to arrive in the evening after an eight-hour trek across western Pennsylvania.

In my carry-on bag is Hannah Pakula's 540-page tome, *The Last Romantic, A Biography of Queen Marie of Romania*. (Queen Marie was the mother of Princess Ileana, the last Romanian princess.) One should not bring books that weigh a ton on travel excursions. (The book's print is too small, so the reading is strenuous. I should have brought a magnifying glass, but as it turned out the book stayed mainly in my bag.)

The western Pennsylvania landscape is quite spectacular. As the train rounds the famous Horseshoe Curve, there's a big to-do; the engineer goes into the history of the curve, which includes a lot of World War Two data as well as how many people died during its construction.

In the café car—I'm traveling business class, so non-alcoholic drinks are on the house—I sit near several Amish people, an Amtrak engineer, a conductor, and a man with an old Bible set beside his coffee. Everybody is engaged in conversation. I jump in at an appropriate time and offer my two cents. The topic is scripture. The man with the Bible is telling stories about how American evangelical Christians, when they see him reading the Bible openly in European settings, always make a loud show of meeting another believer: "O brother in Christ! Another brother in Christ! Let me join you, brother! Can we pray together?" The loudness, of course, is a typically American thing.

The intruders never consider that the man with the Bible might want to be alone. That he might not want to be interrupted because he likes his solitude. But Americans in Europe are like that. They are always the loudest. This is something I became aware of years ago while traveling through France with a married couple. During a train ride into the countryside to visit the George Sand estate, when the husband began speaking in a loud voice his French-educated wife berated him and told him to speak in a whisper.

"You sound like the ugly American," she said. "The French whisper in trains."

Back to the café car, and the man with the Bible is complaining about the Church of England, saying how far it has strayed from apostolic tradition in the last thirty years. I tell him he is speaking the truth. The Amish folk nod in agreement. In the seat behind me is the leader of a Lancaster Amish community. He tells me his small group is traveling to his son's wedding in Indiana. They will change trains in Chicago.

"Isn't it true that some Amish communities are allowed to use cell phones?" I ask.

The leader says the most liberal Amish communities in the country can be found in Lancaster. "I'm not talking about political or theological issues," he assures me, "but things like cell phone ownership."

"So the Amish are nearly all Republican?" I ask. "Absolutely," he answers.

The Amish woman sitting across from me is in a starched black dress with a hundred or so buttons and all kinds of flaps that seem to mimic the religious habit of a monastic. I immediately think of Mother Alexandra—the last princess—while also going back in my mind's eye to the nuns of my childhood—Catholic nuns in traditional habits, not the ones in makeup and skirts.

The train swivels and jerks as it stops at another small Pennsylvania town. "So what do you do?" the leader of the Lancaster community asks. "I'm a writer and author, and I'm going to Pittsburgh and then Ellwood City to do research on the last princess of Romania."

"The what?" somebody in the group says. I give the group a synopsis of Princess Ileana's life. The Amish people want to hear more.

What I give them amounts to a Wikipedia-style overview:
This great-granddaughter of Queen Victoria and relative of Tsar Nicholas II of Russia lived the royal high life in Europe, playing with the Tsar's son, Alexei, on royal yachts but also helping her mother, Queen Marie, attend to the dying and wounded during World War One. She married the Archduke of Austria and had six children; went into another marriage after that and was then told by the communists who invaded her country: either leave or be executed. She took her children first to Switzerland, then to Argentina and then, because she was beginning to have health problems, to the United States to a suburb of Boston, Newton, where—because of the beauty of the New England countryside— she decided to raise her children.

The princess chose Boston because it was a major medical hub, yet there was still a problem: she had to find a house to finish raising her children. When she left Romania, she brought something her mother had given her as a wedding gift in 1931: a sapphire and diamond tiara, a gift from Nicholas I, Emperor of All Russia, to his wife, the former Princess Charlotte of Prussia. Although she pawned the tiara several times to meet financial obligations, the priceless treasure remained safe in Switzerland and then Argentina, but when she went through U.S. Customs she wrapped it in one of her nightgowns.

When she sold the crown, she was able to pay the rest of her debts in Argentina, bring the rest of her family to the United States, pay for the schooling of her children, and—most importantly—buy a house in Newton, Massachusetts, for her family. She did this with the help of then Senator John F. Kennedy—who resided at 122 Bowdoin Street, 36, on Boston's Beacon Hill—who made it possible for her to remain in the country until she became a U.S. citizen.

As Ileana wrote in her memoirs:

> Anxious, weary, in pain [from arthritis], but strangely hopeful, I finally arrived in Miami, where the long flight was interrupted. I lined up for customs inspection, glad to see that no word of my arrival had preceded me on this ... entrance into the United States. I had not realized how public the inspection would be, and when it was my turn and I answered that I had something to declare, I asked if I could unpack my bag in private. The officer was good humored, but a little impatient with my hesitation. When I insisted on it, he made it clear that he thought I was being a nuisance.
>
> "What have you got there, anyway—a corpse?" he asked me.
>
> However, when he finally led me to an office and I opened my bag, it was my turn to feel a little superior. It was obvious that he did not know quite what to do when a tiara turned up in the baggage he inspected. He touched the central sapphire a little gingerly. Since it weighted 125 carats it was nearly the size of a man's pocket watch. Was it real? he wanted to know. When I assured him that it was, he looked still more harassed, but finally he decided that he would send it to Boston "in bond." Together we wrapped it in a newspaper and put it into a box, which he duly sealed and ticketed. It was with a qualm, I confess, that I watched it put into the luggage compartment of the plane for Boston before I myself embarked. If it should somehow be lost, I was losing everything I had, and it was now out of my hands!

When I returned to my seat in the train, it was nearing sunset. The light outside had a hypnotic effect, turning the western Pennsylvania hills into a sort of Transylvania—at least this is what the princess remarked when she saw the Pennsylvania countryside for the first time. It reminded her of the hills and small mountains of Transylvania, and it was for this reason she decided the area was suitable to build a monastery.

Pittsburgh's Union Station is an architectural wreck. Passengers alight from trains 1930s-style, which means climbing down train steps rather than transitioning onto a same-level platform. The station is just one big room with bright fluorescent lights and vending machines. Utilitarian and ugly, it is definitely not worthy of a city with a magnificent skyline known the world over as The Golden Triangle.

Pittsburgh's bridges have a fairyland quality to them that contrasts nicely with the houses, buildings, and onion-domed churches perched on the hills surrounding the downtown area. In many ways, Philadelphia's flat topography cannot match this singing, striking landscape.

Pittsburgh has made many "best lists" since the year 2000. *Forbes* magazine rates Pittsburgh as the nation's most livable city. Pittsburgh beat out Honolulu, which was rated number two. The Farmers Insurance Group also voted Pittsburgh as third on a list of ten of the "Most Secure Places to live in the United States."

The city is ranked among the smartest in the nation. It has been called a city of bookworms despite being a major sports town. It has the best hospitals in the country and the most affordable housing, causing many to refer to it as a "hidden gem." Indeed, when travelers think of Pennsylvania, they tend to think only of Philadelphia. Yet *The Economist* has rated Pittsburgh as the most livable city in the United States.

However, Pittsburgh is not really a Northeastern city at all; it is primarily a Midwestern city, then an Appalachian city, and only lastly something of a Northeastern city—but only somewhat.

At Union Station, I said good-bye to my Amish friends and headed to the arrival area lined with Ubers and taxis. Somewhere in the mix was my ride to the monastery. Emmanuel, the caretaker at Transfiguration, was due to pick me up and drive me the 40 miles or so to Ellwood City. On the phone, Emmanuel described himself as tall and lanky with a long, dark ponytail. Suddenly, a young man fitting that description seemed to jump out of the shadows. We spotted one another instantly.

"Over here," he said, pointing to a small SUV parked on the far side of the ramp. Within minutes we were on the road to Ellwood. Small talk soon turned into serious conversation about the monastery, the nuns, the last princess, and Emmanuel's time at Transfiguration as assistant caretaker.

Emmanuel asked about Philadelphia. Overall, he had a reserve fairly uncommon for men his age. Of Greek descent, one of his close relatives was a priest, and he mentioned serving with him at Divine

Liturgy as a tonsured Reader. He said he lived in an apartment near the monastery and was "well compensated" for his work.

During the ride to St. Bridget's monastery guesthouse, where I would be staying, it occurred to me that Emmanuel resembled Prince Anton of Austria, the man whom biographers say Princess Ileana was more or less forced to marry by her elder brother, King Carol. King Carol had a rather low opinion of the princess—he once called her base and conniving—and he wanted her out of Romania. He himself had twice abdicated succession to the throne, once when he went off to marry and live with his mistress, Elena Lupescu. Later he announced he was giving up Elena—he did not keep this promise—and through a series of Byzantine mechanizations he eventually worked his way back to the throne.

Ileana had always been close to her brother, and once he was back on the throne, Carol took it for granted she would support him in his feud with his wife, Princess Helen. Ileana, however, supported Princess Helen (Sitta) rather than her brother's mistress, and that did not sit well with the king, who immediately punished her by removing her from the presidency of the Y.W.C.A. and the Girl Scouts.

Yet things did not end there. Carol found a way to force Ileana out of Romania altogether.

Hannah Pakula writes in *The Last Romantic, A Biography of Queen Marie of Romania*:

> Looking for a way to rid himself of this "aching thorn" in his side and remembering Anton of Austria, Carol decided to marry Ileana off. He contacted Prince Friedrich, Head of the House of Hohenzollern-Sigmaringen, and his wife and asked them to invite Ileana and Anton to Umrich. "We found that there were many things we had in common," Ileana recalled many years later. "We liked flying and we got on very well. It was a sort of rebound thing … I never realized the trap I was walking into, or else I might have thought twice about it."

Queen Marie's concerns about the marriage had nothing to do with Anton's pedigree, which was flawless. But there was a fly in the ointment—it's called ruined aristocracy. Pakula continues:

But Anton was a penniless exile. After the family fled Austria, he had earned his living working in a gas station in Spain. Marie felt that of all her children, Ileana was best-suited to wear a crown. A decent, kindly young man, more comfortable in workman's overalls than formal dress, Anton had had little time or opportunity for an education. "So there are great lapses in his knowledge of art, literature and ... history," Marie said. "But he's an expert engineer and electrician, and a first rate pilot. Big, solid, trustworthy, he has not a penny except what he earns with his own hands."

King Carol believed forcing Ileana to marry an Austrian would assure the couple's move to Austria, because the Romanian people would never tolerate a Habsburg living in their country. Ileana and Anton's wedding took place on July 26, 1931. It was a sad affair, with the princess's mother, Queen Marie, in tears and the princess herself sobbing as she knelt before the queen in ceremonial fashion after the nuptials. The princess, who loved Romania, knew her marriage meant exile and separation from the Romanian people.

The Brothers Grimm fairy tale picture of a prince with no money pumping gas taps into the notion of "ruined aristocracy," when people of noble lineage retain the class and manners of their heritage but no longer have the cash to support it. One thinks of the lives of American socialite Edith Ewing Bouvier Beale and daughter Edith Bouvier Beale in the rundown, cat- and raccoon-infested East Hampton estate (and film), Grey Gardens.

"Follow that little bridge if you want to see Mother Alexandra's grave," Emmanuel said, interrupting my thoughts and indicating a small wooden bridge near the entrance to Transfiguration.

I told myself I would visit the grave the following day after getting settled in at St. Bridget's House, the small house where the princess spent her last years. A number of guest houses, a chapel, the central monastery area, and nuns' quarters lined the long road that cut through the middle of Transfiguration. St. Bridget's House was the last building before the beginning of a dense wooded area. Emmanuel gave me a quick tour of the house. My eyes went directly to a small but substantial library in the living room, where I would soon find several of the princess's books (signed "Ileana,

1956," not "Mother Alexandra"). Before Emmanuel departed, I reached into my pocket for a tip, but he reminded me that he was "well compensated."

This was the princess's last house, the house where she recuperated after breaking her hip but also where she had her office in the living room. Old photos on the wall showed a large desk placed before the picture window that looked out over fields, woods, and mountainous hills beyond. Transylvania! I imagined the princess pacing back and forth, gazing out onto the same landscape I was looking at.

In this room, the princess no doubt pondered the wide scope of her life; when, as a child, she had played and swam at the beach with Alexei, son of Tsar Nicholas II of Russia. In the famous photo of Alexei and Ileana in which she is clutching Alexei's arm, her girlish smile is buried in a head of curls. She comes across as a kind of Romanian Shirley Temple, while Alexei—his eyes slanted leftward—seems focused on someone or something happening behind the camera.

The founding of the Orthodox Monastery of the Transfiguration was the dream of Ileana, who was tonsured a nun in 1968 at the Monastery of the Veil in Bussy, France. Separated from her former life as a princess—all of her six children were now grown up—she began making plans for an idea she had about building an American monastery. She did not know where the monastery would be, but she wanted a Pan-Orthodox monastery—whether Greek, Russian, Bulgarian, or Romanian—with services in English.

In the French monastery, she began working on English translations of the daily liturgical services in the Orthodox Church, such as the Lenten Triodion and the Festal Menaion. At that time there were no Orthodox monasteries for women in the United States. Even among the various Orthodox churches, the concept of religious women living together in a monastery was viewed as something only Catholics do. When the princess-nun attempted to canvass Orthodox clergy and potential donors for funds to build Transfiguration, she encountered surprised and shocked reactions: "That's not Orthodox," she was told.

It was suggested if she wanted to found a monastery for nuns, she needed to go over to the Catholic Church.

Orthodoxy got a late start establishing communities for women monastics in the United States. Roman Catholic nuns had been in the United States since the eighteenth century. Mother Bernardina Teresa Xavier of St. Joseph (1732–1800) established the first Catholic convent in America in 1790. An American by birth, Mother Bernardina spent time in England before returning to America with three fellow Discalced (shoeless) Carmelite nuns to find the convent of Mt. Carmel in Port Tobacco, Maryland.

In 1852, the first Catholic Benedictine nuns arrived in the United States from St. Walburga Abbey in Eichstätt, Germany. They settled in St. Mary's, Pennsylvania, and soon established several foundations, including one at Erie, Pennsylvania, and later St. Walburg Monastery in Kentucky.

"I am a hopeless optimist," Mother Alexandra told a newspaper reporter in 1968. "It is very difficult to discourage me. I really believe this is what God wants me to do, so I dare not fail."

Ileana elaborated on her idea of a monastery in the mid-1960s while a member of the community in Bussy, France:

> Work has always been deemed an integral part of prayer, thus the convent of the Transfiguration proposes to print books, paint icons, make church vestments; it will accept young and old to partake in its liturgical life and in general to busy itself with the spiritual needs of all the faithful. It can also become a center for receiving members of other confessions who are interested in the Orthodox way of life. An appropriate place for the convent is being searched for, where quietly and without interruption, the monastic tradition of life and prayer may continue.

Ground for the monastery was purchased in 1965, two years before the princess's tonsure when she became Sister Ileana. Fundraising was difficult, with some of it ($1,000) coming from the princess's own savings. A list of initial donors appeared in the first issue of the monastery journal, *Life Transfigured*. Donations poured in from all over the United States, ranging from $5 to $9,000.

Finally, in 1968, *The Beaver Valley Times* reported the Orthodox Monastery of the Transfiguration was nearing completion.

"Dream to Reality," the story's headline ran; "Monastery Dream of Former Princess Becomes a Reality." The article continued:

> Of chalet design, the new building is constructed of prefabricated redwood and is located on a gentle slope in wooded land overlooking Slippery Rock Creek. Estimated cost of the building is $70,000. When completed the monastery will consist of a chapel that rises in the middle of a complex of 12 cells, reception rooms, office, kitchen, utility rooms, and garage.

Prior to the opening of the monastery in Ellwood City and the consecration of the chapel, the princess lived in a trailer on monastery grounds. The trailer was one of a series of homes Ileana inhabited before she was able to move into the newly constructed residence. Initially she lived with her son in Farmington, Michigan, and then with an Orthodox priest and his wife in Ellwood City before the arrival of the life-saving trailer.

In a letter to Mother Eudoxia, Abbess of the Monastery of the Veil in Bussy, in May 1968, Ileana shared some of her experiences of getting settled:

> This is my first letter from the Monastery grounds. I wish I had Mama's [Queen Marie of Romania] gift for description and also the time to write about all we have been doing and the excitement of our move up here! It is so very beautiful just now, all fresh green, and the apple blossom's out ... Our trailer nestles, if one can use such an expression for anything so big, right in among the trees. The getting up of it here was a whole saga. We left early from Toronto [Ohio] assured that the trailer would follow us in two hours. ... Then Fr. Useriu turned up, saying the Pennsylvania Police would not let the thing through, so off I dashed with him ... and I went to the police who were very nice and telephoned all over the place. Well to make a long story short we got a police escort for the trailer from the Ohio border through Ellwood ... It really was a sight: two police cars with flashing lights, a little truck with lights, and behind it the trailer; we parted from the police, turned on our lights and escorted our home to its place ... They placed it in its location in no time, BUT no one else kept their word so we had no water, and no light, and of course

no heat and the weather took a dip to 32 degrees. Happily we did have gas for cooking and so hot water and of course any amount of candles.

On September 28, 1968, the consecration of the monastery's altar took place with hundreds in attendance, including two nuns from the convent in Bussy. Previously, a temporary chapel had been erected inside the trailer. The day—as reported by *Life Transfigured*—"dawned somewhat cloudy with a slight drizzle, but soon the mist and clouds rolled away, and we were blessed with bright, sun-drenched weather for the entire day."

After the celebration of a Pontifical Divine Liturgy and the installation of Ileana as abbess, a picnic luncheon was served.

2

Meeting the Nuns

I skipped early-morning services my first day at Transfiguration, but headed over to the dining room to meet Mother Paula, the guest master who arranged my stay, and to share a midday lunch. Mother Paula entered the monastery in 2010. Of Greek descent, she told me that prior to entering monastic life she used to be an elementary school teacher. After graciously inquiring how my first night in St. Bridget's House was, Mother Paula ushered me into the chapel for the Liturgy of the Hours. The service began without a priest, the nuns' choir comprising ten nuns with a visiting nun from Alaska, and was over in less than an hour. Afterwards, Mother Paula escorted me back into the chapel and pointed out an icon of Christ on the iconostasis, a gift from Tsar Nicholas II. On the other side of the Royal Doors, she indicated an icon of the Virgin that once belonged to Queen Marie. Mother Paula said the queen used to hold the icon before Romanian troops prior to their going to war.

The Nicholas II icon of Christ was especially compelling: Who had touched it, I wondered. Had it ever fallen into the hands of Grigori Yefimovich Rasputin? Had it ever been placed by the bedside of Tsarevich Alexei Nikolaevich? I ran my fingers across the top of the icon, desiring to physically connect with history.

The large Oriental carpet in the main part of the chapel was also a gift from Tsar Nicholas II. Although a little threadbare in places, its condition overall was remarkably well preserved. How had the tsar chosen the carpet? Did he purchase it new or had it been used in the Alexander Palace in St. Petersburg?

I followed Mother Paula throughout the monastery as she pointed out various items of interest: the princess's chair where she sat as abbess; her staff; a collection of plateware with the family crest from the royal yacht; silverware (also from the tsar). We entered the dining room through a "nuns only" entrance for expediency's sake, a route I would take the following day only to be reminded by a rule-oriented young nun that the passageway was for "the sisters only." By this point I had gotten extremely chatty with Mother Paula, so I felt comfortable asking her if in her former life she was ever married. The next day this question would come back to haunt me when Mother Paula reminded me I should never ask the nuns if they were married before they entered the monastery.

Indeed, one should ask the nuns nothing about their lives before they entered the monastery. As I would later discover through my contact with Mother Elizabeth (Carol Bacha) of Palm Coast, Florida, who was Mother Alexandra's young assistant shortly after the founding of Transfiguration, "When I was first there in 1974, Ileana's policy was we don't show family pictures, pictures of ourselves, and no questions about your background."

Yet asking the same question to Catholic or Orthodox monks was always an effortless task. In fact, monks always seemed eager to talk about their past lives, especially the ones who have radical "before" and "after" conversion stories.

"I'm prone to ask a lot of questions myself, so I understand how you as a journalist might do this without thinking," Mother Paula cautioned. She was trying to be diplomatic, of course. I concurred, complimenting her on how comfortable she made me feel about asking questions that might be outside the box while also stating I had not yet asked any of the other nuns whether or not they ever had a husband. Mother Alexandra, after all—as a desirable young princess—had two husbands, Archduke Anton of Austria, Prince of Tuscany, and later Dr. Stefan Nicolaus Issarescu, a pathologist.

Archduke Anton was born in 1901 in Vienna, the seventh of ten children born to Leopold Salvator of Austria. During World War Two, while married to Ileana, he served in the German Wehrmacht as a pilot. When Romania's alliance with Germany ended in 1944, he and Ileana—realizing their family was in danger of imprisonment— lived on borrowed time until the official abdication of Romania's

King Michael I in December 1947, at which point, as we have seen, they fled to Switzerland, then Argentina, and finally to the United States. (Anton and Ileana were officially divorced in 1954.)

More than 300 guests attended Ileana's wedding to Archduke Anton in the Romanian mountain resort of Sinaia. The day before the event—July 25, 1931—it had snowed, so some of the marriage festivities were cancelled. In a letter to a friend, Queen Marie described Anton as "big, solid, trustworthy, he has not a penny except what he earns with his own hand." It was a harsh judgment, perhaps more relevant to the times than to posterity because I would get a very different take on Anton—and his relationship with both Ileana and Queen Marie—when I interviewed Dominic Habsburg, Ileana's only surviving son, in his home near Purdys, New York, in October 2024.

Despite the frosty weather leading up to Ileana's marriage, the full guest list included Ileana's two sisters, Queen Elizabeth of the Hellenes and Queen Marie of Yugoslavia. The young Crown Prince Michael of Romania also attended, as did Ileana's maternal aunt, Grand Duchess Victoria Melita, and various members of Archduke Anton's family.

Ileana wore a diamond tiara and a gown of white *crepe de chine* with silver embroidery. *The New York Times* mistakenly reported that the Orthodox Patriarch—which Orthodox Patriarch it did not say—had gone to Sinaia to bless Ileana before her conversion to Roman Catholicism, since Anton was Catholic. The *Times* also stated that two Catholic bishops had been sent to Sinaia by the Vatican to baptize Ileana into the Catholic faith before the ceremony.

These reports could not have been further from the truth. Ileana not only remained Orthodox, she never had any intention of converting to Catholicism. The report of a new baptism was especially erroneous, since Ileana had already been baptized as an Orthodox Christian, making a second baptism not only unnecessary but an abuse of a sacrament recognized as valid by both Churches. Ileana, however, did promise to raise her children Roman Catholic. To solidify that promise, she and Anton made a trip to Rome to meet Pope Pius XI and then sign a document to that effect. (Pope Pius XI was the first pope to specifically address the Christian ecumenical movement; he was also extremely interested in achieving reunion with the Eastern Orthodox Church, and during his reign he gave special attention to the Eastern Catholic churches.)

Ironically, both of Ileana's marriages ended in divorce. With Anton she had six children: Archduke Stefan of Austria, Archduchess Maria Ileana of Austria ("Minola"), Archduchess Alexandra of Austria ("Sandi"), Archduke Dominic of Austria ("Niki"), Archduchess Maria Magdalena of Austria ("Magi"), and Archduchess Elisabeth of Austria ("Herzi").

In a blog entitled *The Romanov Family*, Helen Azar writes:

Ileana and her husband were largely estranged when she had an affair with one of the local senior communist officials, who helped her keep her hospital open. But by late 1947, this was no longer possible and Ileana was told it was over, and she and her family were driven out of the new communist Romania. They eventually settled in Switzerland, then moved to Argentina, and in 1950 Ileana and her children moved to the United States, and settled in Newton, Massachusetts.

In 1954, Ileana and Anton officially divorced, and later that year she got married for the second time to Dr. Stefan Nicolaus Issarescu. In 1961, with her children grown, Princess Ileana decided to enter the Convent of the Intercession of the Mother of God in Bussy, France—before her divorce from Dr. Issarescu, which occurred a few years later—where she was given the name Sister Alexandra.

Standing at Ileana's grave, just a short walk from the general monastery, I was struck by the top layer of white pebbles covering the site. Stones or pebbles are common Jewish grave markers, symbolizing a show of respect for the deceased; they also serve as an indicator that someone has visited the gravesite. Yet the princess was not Jewish. Perhaps the pebbles were merely a utilitarian way to save mowing the grass or frame the grave in a special way that made it stand out from the others.

The name on the headstone cross, Mother Alexandra-Princess Ileana, suggested the famed abbess never forgot she was a princess. This dual identity—many monastics, as my exchange with Mother Paula showed, seemed to put their former lives or what "they once were" in the dustbin of the forgettable—would come into play in a larger sense during my conversation with Dominic Habsburg, but more about that later.

Standing at the gravesite, I thought of taking a stone or two as a memento, the way one would take something that had touched the body of a saint; my version of an unofficial relic. But Mother Alexandra was not a saint, at least not officially. Still, taking a pebble might prove to have some significance—a relic not yet holy—and yet I could not do it. The flip side of the coin in pocketing a pebble might be desecration. What if every visitor pocketed a pebble? They would all be gone, thanks to selfish tourist "religiosity."

An old woman stood before another grave not too far from where I was standing. She did not seem to notice me; her full attention seemed to be on her prayers. I left the cemetery after a little while and proceeded to walk among the fields and trees that encompass the monastery's 96 acres. I imagined Ileana taking in the same view almost fifty years ago. A small bench in front of a tree facing a statue of the Crucifixion seemed a good place to sit and let my mind wonder. No sooner had I settled on the bench when in the distance I noticed a nun walking in the field nearest the chapel. The nun had a pale-colored wide-brim hat on top of her veil. She was alone and walking far into the field; I watched as she went out into the field and then circled back towards the monastery. She was too far away for me to recognize a face, yet for an instant the sight reminded me of a scene out of an old movie.

Earlier that day, after lunch, one of the younger nuns who had been washing dishes walked by me with a Pittsburgh Steelers hat on top of her veil. It was the same nun who had corrected me for walking down the wrong hallway. Ah, I thought, she has a sense of humor after all. Just another example of how underneath the religious habits and the attention to daily prayer and services, these are normal women after all.

My interview with Mother Christophora, the current Abbess of Transfiguration, was due to take place after my walk in the fields.

Raised in an Orthodox family in northeastern Pennsylvania and educated at Penn State University (after which she became an addictions counselor and program administrator), Mother Christophora entered Transfiguration at age 29.

At that time, Mother Benedicta (1978–1986) was abbess, having taken over the reins from Mother Alexandra when she retired due to failing health. In many books and articles about Ileana, there are paragraphs devoted to the tremendous act of humility it took for Mother Alexandra to renounce the office of abbess and hand it over to a younger nun, especially when—at least according to Dominic Habsburg—the abbess who abdicated had an "I am" personality in which she expected each of her children to be extensions of herself rather than unique individuals who had a life path of their own to follow.

The "I am" personality might be described in some way by quoting E. B. White when he wrote that the essay writer especially is

> a self-liberated man, sustained by the childish belief that everything he thinks about, everything that happens to him, is of general interest … Only a person who is congenitally self-centered has the effrontery and the stamina to write essays.

Furthermore, White stated, "I think some people … feel that it is presumptuous of a writer to assume his little excursions or his small observations will interest the reader." The same might be said of a great visionary, leader, saint, or artist. Indeed, as the great-granddaughter of Queen Victoria, a woman who had to protect her family during the downfall of her beloved Romania to communism, who founded a great hospital—Hospital of the Queen's Heart—during World War Two, and who had to reinvent herself after her expulsion from Romania, Ileana was a life force with an ego some might say contained a bit of a "God complex." She can be partially understood, I think, in Michelangelo's famous quote: "I saw the angel in the marble and carved until I set him free."

Ileana's first book, *I Live Again* (1951), a memoir of her life before and after her role of abbess at the Monastery of the Transfiguration, was followed by *Hospital of the Queen's Heart* (1954), about the hospital she founded in the Romanian town of Bran. In 1981, she published *The Holy Angels*, an account of the history of angels in both the Hebrew Bible and the New Testament and the role they play in the salvation of humankind.

Turning over the reins of power to Mother Benedicta—who was born and raised in Romania, living in the Voroneţ Monastery there since she was a child and emigrating to the United States to assist Ileana in the founding of Transfiguration—was not an easy task for Ileana. A fairly young abbot or abbess may present issues to older monks and nuns in monasteries under their direction.

At St. Tikhon's monastery in Waymart, Pennsylvania, I briefly got to know an older Serbian monk who seemed to have an air of discontent about him. My sense was he was struggling with something internal. Not only did he not have the "settled down and content" look of the other monks, but at times he appeared overtly annoyed with some issue, whether real or imagined. When I finally had a chance to talk with him about his life before and after entering monastic life—he had a long career as a chef in several five-star restaurants prior to taking vows—he told me the main issue was being under the authority of an abbot much younger than he.

This of course would involve obedience and taking orders from a younger man who in many ways might be perceived as not having the life experience of the older man. The day after our conversation, I spotted the Serbian monk clearing out small dead trees and underbrush from a wooded part of the monastery that the abbot probably wanted cleared. He worked with what I can only describe as an agitated energy; one imagined him cursing silently as he threw branches this way and that. He looked totally fed up. Seeing this, I recalled his comments about the younger abbot.

Not privy to any particulars—he could merely have been one of those highly strung personality types who appear agitated no matter what they do—it was fairly obvious the task was an assignment he did not like. A year later, when I returned to St. Tikhon's for another retreat, I was informed that the Serbian monk had found a happy new home in a Serbian monastery out west—hopefully under the direction of an elderly abbot.

As the third abbess of the monastery, Mother Christophora and I were to meet in the monastery library. As a prelude to the conversation, Mother Paula showed me a Pittsburgh TV news clip on Transfiguration and an interview with Mother Alexandra conducted in the 1980s. The newscaster, an enthusiastic, healthy-looking woman with big Eighties hair, kept emphasizing the abbess's life as a former princess. While watching the news clip, Mother Paula informed me the newscaster had died of cancer some years ago, yet here she was in the prime of life, not thinking of death but enjoying her Pittsburgh television career.

I rose when Mother Christophora entered the room, noticing right away that here was a woman who commanded the kind of respect you would give a head of state or diplomat.

I began the conversation by stating I had interviewed another Orthodox nun, Mother Elizabeth in Palm Coast, Florida, who told me a lot about Mother Alexandra, based on her experience at Transfiguration when she was the former princess's assistant.

Mother Christophora said:

I'm here 41 years as a sister. I've been abbess since 1987. I was 29 when I came here though I started coming here in 1981 and joined in '83. By that time Mother Alexandra had retired; Mother Benedicta was in charge of the monastery. Mother Benedicta entered the monastery at age 9 in Romania.

Growing up in a monastery is a rare phenomenon, but Saint Agnes of Montepulciano, Tuscany, had entered the Monastery of the Dominican Nuns of the Second Order—also known as the "Sisters of the Sack" because of the coarse habits they wore—at the age of 9. While Mother Benedicta did not take vows at age 9, she more or less lived the life of a nun as a young girl.

I asked Mother Christophora if she was aware of a current theory believed by many that some members of the Russian royal family had survived the assassination of 1918, namely the tsar's daughters and wife, as well as son Alexei. Alexei, Mother Elizabeth of Palm Coast had informed me, had escaped and later changed his name when he migrated to the United States, married and started working for the United Nations. She added that he was buried behind the Serbian Orthodox cathedral in Belgrade. To that effect, Mother Elizabeth told me she had in her possession an ID card with Alexei's new name on it. (At the time of my interview with Mother Elizabeth, she said the card was "somewhere in my house.")

"Well," Mother Christophora answered, not seeming shocked or bothered by the theory, "I do remember when people would just show up. People would come here and claim that they were so and so." Who did she mean, I wondered.

She then named two American women who were young nuns when Mother Alexandra was abbess: Sister Catherine (now Mother Cassiana Petrow of Lake George, Colorado) and Mother Dominica. "Mother Cassiana would know things I don't know because she lived here before I came," Mother Christophora said.

"My grandparents came from Eastern Europe. I grew up in Wilkes Barre, Pennsylvania, went to college, worked seven years, joined here; I was 29 or something in 1983," Mother Christophora added, seeming to break the taboo of talking about her past, going on to speak of Ileana:

> When I got here she just looked so old to me. I only knew her as a nun. The first time I saw her was at St. Tikhon's monastery in the early 1970s. We were standing right across from her. She was an imposing figure ... her cross was precise and her posture perfect.

We talked about the artifacts in the monastery from the princess's life in Romania. "There are a few plates from Ileana's yacht and some silver from the tsar." There was also the icon of Christ in the chapel, of course, but where was the wooden statue of Saint Benedict?

The statue is mentioned in Ileana's book, *I Live Again*, as one of the important items she took with her after her expulsion from Romania:

> We were permitted to take only personal belongings—that is to say, clothes, linen, and silver for the use of eight people—but no works of art, as these were "the property of the people," no carpets, and no jewels except those which were indisputably "family jewels" not acquired in recent years. A Control Commission came to watch us carefully so that we should "steal" none of our property—two men in Bucharest and eighteen men in Bran [the royal castle]. These men were with us continually, so that there was no question of privacy, even for discussion. They were still to some extent human, so that at my pleading they did make an occasional exception: it is for that reason the statue of St. Benedict stands today in my bedroom, after having been smuggled out "by permission" in window draperies.

Mother Christophora confirmed that Ileana had the statue of St. Benedict in her bedroom in St. Bridget's House and that in her will it was to go to one of her children, but she did not know which child. Later, I discovered that it went to Dominic Habsburg, Ileana's sole surviving son, when I traveled to his home in Purdys, New York. The question of the statue brought up other family members.

Mother Christophora continued:

Stefan [Ileana's eldest son] worked for General Motors in Michigan, but he and his wife passed away. Niki [Dominic] was in touch with the monastery after she died. He didn't visit Mother Alexandra when she lived here. He was a little less chummy than the other kids. I think there may have been a power struggle.

Just what the abbess was talking about would make sense to me after my long conversation with Dominic Habsburg some weeks after I left Transfiguration. Dominic talked about his relationship with his mother, stressing her "I am" personality with his need for independence and not wanting his life to be "an extension" of hers or what she expected from her children. He would also tell me that his grandmother (Queen Marie) and mother both felt they were superior to men.

Mother Christophora continued:

Mother Alexandra went to Europe for a month every year with her children. They'd visit Salzburg, Austria, and Stefan and his family came to the monastery a lot. Mother Alexandra also went to Michigan a lot. Regarding Niki, he inherited Bran Castle. This was when Romania was giving back property to former owners. The other children didn't want the castle. Niki turned it into a tourist attraction.

Google searches on Bran Castle will produce images of Dracula, cobwebs, and other low-rent "spooky" images from the castle's interior. The images have nothing to do with real horror or terror; it is camp horror as seen through the eyes of a high school sophomore. "Princess Ileana must be spinning in her grave," I thought, reviewing them.

"Is Halloween at Bran Castle worth it?" Reddit asks. There are blogs offering travel guides to Bran Castle's Halloween Party. "Unveiling the Spooktacular," one advertisement states. Other sites advertise the price of Bran Castle Halloween tickets. Spooktacular in particular notes:

> For the weekend celebrations, Bran Castle is given a spooky "make-over" to enhance the Halloween experience. Inside, there are dressed up actors available for photos, Halloween decorations throughout the castle, and a few jump scares. It gives a similar vibe to Disney's Halloween setup and celebration. On the outside, there's a spooky projector casting images onto the castle, and moody lighting around the grounds.

According to Mother Elizabeth of Palm Coast, who worked as Ileana's assistant, Ileana was dead set against the "Dracula-ization" of Bran Castle. "Not in my castle!" Ileana reportedly said of this turn of events. But what could she do? The overhype of Halloween and adolescent theatrical horror seems to attract plenty of devotees fixated on papier-mâché imitations of the vampire that jump out of dark corners and shout "Boo!" at tourists. It is bad enough that Halloween is being turned into a holiday on a par with Thanksgiving and Christmas, but idolizing "Trick or Treat" costumes and camp horror in this most noble of castles does not even come close to the real horror the walls of Bran—if they could talk—have witnessed.

"As I have indicated, the Communist Party early in 1945 began coming out into the open, agitating strikes and putting on 'manifestations' which were protected and sustained by the Russian troops," Ileana wrote in *I Live Again*. Romania's old alliance with Nazi Germany was now broken and a new form of fascism was about to take hold. The establishment of a Russian-dominated Romanian government was solidified on March 6, 1945 when Petru Groza—described by Ileana as a "windbag and opportunist"—was declared the nation's premier. Ileana goes on to describe the hospital she founded—the Hospital of the Queen's Heart—as the beginning of open persecutions.

In January 1945, she adds, it was declared that "all citizens of German origin were to be deported to Russia ... All men between the ages of seventeen and forty-five and all women between eighteen and thirty, whether or not they had children, were to be taken at once."

Ileana writes of Russian troops "ruthlessly dragging men and women from their homes," while "mothers were separated from their weeping children, husbands and sons from their wives and parents; young girls from their families. There were heartrending scenes; scenes that made one's blood boil. And one could do nothing—nothing!"

Was the "Dracula-ization" of Bran Castle Dominic Habsburg's fault? The Bran Castle website states:

On May 18, 2009, after 61 years, 4 months and 11 days of state ownership, the Bran Castle was returned to the children of Princess Ileana of Romania, Dominic, Elisabeth and Maria Magdalena. All traces of the family had been eliminated. What once was Queen Marie's most cherished residence, and our family home, was stripped and barren.

Within three weeks, the Bran Castle was restored, blooming in full splendor, to welcome you.

Four years later, the Bran Castle has become a destination for over 500,000 visitors each year who can delight in countless activities such as music festivals, children's pageants, and food fairs. Recognizing that Bran was the inspiration for Dracula's Castle in the Bram Stoker's celebrated novel, *Dracula*, visitors can enjoy rooms dedicated to Transylvania's most famous count ... and, in the coming months, dine in Queen Marie's Tea House and ride a glass elevator to experience "Dracula's escape route".

Yet there have been benefits to the remaking of Bran Castle. Mother Christophora mentioned that tourists to Romania who visit the castle are told Princess Ileana became an Orthodox nun and founded a monastery in Pennsylvania. Apparently this fact is still not widely known, but once this information is shared the same tourists often find their way to Ellwood City to see the monastery the princess founded. This is a relatively new development, the abbess stated.

An actress from Romania, Liana Ceterchi, was here in 2018 and gave a one-woman performance of Princess Ileana's life. "Ileana, Princess of Romania" was staged in the dining room. Ceterchi based the play on Mother Alexandra's memoir, *I Live Again*. She did the play in Detroit and Washington DC. You can see the play on YouTube but you have to listen carefully because the English style is to mumble.

Before the sisterhood at Transfiguration grew, Ileana lived alone in a trailer at the monastery, waiting and praying for "recruits." Today, in terms of monastic vocations, the monastery—or any Orthodox women's monastery for that matter—is not seeing a lot of young women who want to follow Ileana's path. Mother Christophora told me:

> Regarding new vocations, it's a tough time. A lot of young men are going into Orthodoxy and monasteries but women have gone into refrigeration ... But look at what the culture is doing to women. A few decades ago there were more nuns than monks.

"Gone into refrigeration"; the abbess's term struck me as odd but somehow appropriate. Where have all the young women gone? Has post-modern, third- or fourth-wave feminism captured their minds, bodies, and spirits?

Carrie Gress, Ph.D. writes in her book, *Something Wicked: Why Feminism Can't Be Fused with Christianity*:

> The gospel of discontent may feel energizing and enlightening, but the one thing it cannot ever provide is real human flourishing. Nothing can be built on that which destroys. Here again, feminism as a movement, which was supposedly built on reason and rationalism, is in the business of basing everything on fleeting and ever changing emotional states....Christian women, like most other women—from Barbara Walters to Taylor Swift—have bought deeply into this gospel of discontent. The malignant voice that has whispered to women for decades is not the still small voice of the Holy Spirit.

In 2013, the abbess gave an interview to Matushka Valerie Zahirsky, which was later published in two parts in the monastery's publication, *Life Transfigured*:

Mother Alexandra was a Romanian princess, part of a royal family that has a centuries-long history. After she had to leave her country, she raised her children and then got to fulfill her dream to become a nun. She was living in America but she went to France to become a nun. She saw our country was very rich materially but very poor spiritually, and she wanted America to have an Orthodox monastery. This was her gift; this was what she did. She gave America an Orthodox monastery, because she knew that it would add to life here. But she did not give America a Romanian Orthodox monastery or a Russian Orthodox monastery or a Greek Orthodox monastery. She gave America an Orthodox monastery for Americans.

In the 1960s when very little English was used in Orthodox churches, she was determined that everything would be in English from day one, that American women of all backgrounds would feel welcome here. I think her dream is being realized and has been realized. She saw that you do not have to be—and we all know this, but it still bears repeating—Greek or Russian or Ukrainian or Serbian to be Orthodox. America needs Orthodoxy. She knew that. We can also, as Americans, be comfortable in the Orthodox Church in our own way. Here we have enjoyed discovering that—like watching petals of a flower open as we live out our monastic life as Americans in this Orthodox monastery.

In *Life Transfigured*, Mother Christophora talked about the single life before entering the monastery. No doubt she spoke for many young women when she stated,

I have observed the single life, and I think, "Wow, that is fun when you are 20 or 30, but as you get to be 50, 60, 70, and you are alone in the world, it is awful to have no support system around you." People that get married have, just naturally, your children, your spouse, some extended family ...

In the monastery, we have a family here, we have each other. In the Christian community, whether it be the community of marriage or the monastic community, there is a lot of support for each other, and it is wonderful. It is when we are isolated and alone that it is very, very hard. The surprise, I guess, would be that I have come to appreciate community life when I thought it would just be "Well, that is just the way it is. I will just have to deal with that. It will not be nice, but it is nice."

* * *

Have patience with everything that remains unsolved in your heart. Try to love the questions themselves, like locked rooms and like books.

—Rainer Maria Rilke

I had an experience in St. Bridget's House concerning Ileana's old bedroom. In the living room there were a set of double wooden doors that led to another part of the house. A posted sign on the left door cautioned against opening it and stated only the right door was to be used. The note suggested free access, so of course I used the right door to see what was behind it. To my surprise, it opened up into an entire bedroom suite and a large bathroom. The bedroom was decorated with pictures and some icons, and the bed was unusually large with an old-fashioned headboard.

I poked around a bit, aware this was where Ileana probably slept but curious as to why it was not being utilized fully, as the other rooms in the house were. I may have closed my eyes for a minute while inspecting the rooms, hoping to feel something of Ileana's spirit or perhaps, upon opening them again, spot an artifact on a bureau top that may have belonged to the princess. But no. It was a void space, uninteresting for the most part, and so I left, exiting through the operable door.

Later that evening, returning from Vespers, I thought I should take another look at the bedroom, thinking I had dismissed it too quickly, when I noticed the note cautioning against using the left door had been removed. I then went to open the right door, but it was locked. How strange. Did Mother Paula tell Emmanuel to lock Ileana's entrance, and if she did, for what reason? Was it because there was something in these rooms I was not supposed to see? The feeling was a little bit like being spied upon, as if somehow Mother Paula had gotten wind that I had gone into the rooms and taken a look. Then it occurred to me that perhaps that was not the case at all, but merely a matter of Mother Paula having remembered that the one door to the bedroom was unlocked and as a matter of "formula" it should always be locked when guests visit.

Still, I could not help but feel that I had been slapped on the wrist, as if the monastery did not trust me. I told myself I would speak to Mother Paula the following day about the doors. Why were they open and then suddenly locked? The next day, when the opportunity presented itself, I did ask Mother Paula about the doors, but she was casual and dismissive, saying the rooms were usually locked and that the bedroom suite had been changed so many times since Ileana's death it retained nothing of its original form. Even the furniture was different, she said.

"I did go in there," I said. "There was a sign on the left door saying to use the right door, so that came across as a green light. Was I not supposed to go in there?"

"Oh no," Mother Paula said, smiling, "everybody likes to snoop. It's natural to see what was in there. Don't think twice about it. People do it all the time." Her making a joke out of it made it harder for me to talk about it further. But doors are usually locked for a reason.

My last evening at Transfiguration began at Vespers, when the nuns said a prayer for my research. Earlier, at the midday meal, I was asked to say a few words about myself. The kind nuns also presented me with two gift books from the bookstore. On my way to St. Bridget's House after these farewells, I was walking near the fields when I spotted the tall nun in the hat I had seen earlier, returning from another walk in the fields. This time, however, I could see who the nun was. It was Mother Christophora, who seemed to be walking towards me.

We exchanged a few words—she wanted to know about Philadelphia and what neighborhood I lived in, while I thanked her for her hospitality. "You've taken on a big project," she said. "I'll pray for you."

The next morning I was up before the crack of dawn, waiting for a Uber driver to pick me up at the monastery's entrance. The car arrived in the pitch black—headlights on—waiting by the side of the driveway not too far from Ileana's grave. I hurried down to meet it. The driver was a middle-aged male and devout evangelical

Christian who engaged me in conversation during the hour's drive into Pittsburgh.

Having picked me up at a monastery, the talk soon turned to religion and churches, especially the Catholic Church and its veneration of statues and images, not to mention the "power" of the pope. The driver had not heard an awful lot about Orthodoxy, so he was clueless when it came to that subject, but at one point he began to raise his voice and preach against the abuses of traditional apostolic Christianity, namely Catholicism, while insisting that scripture and not the baggage of "The Church' was the only thing needed for salvation.

As he made certain points, he would accelerate. I opted to let him speak and rant, fearing an argument would result in an accident. As we neared Pittsburgh—the view from my window was unspectacular, as it had been on my arrival some days before—he had calmed down and was now apologizing for overdoing things. I told him it was okay, that the main thing was a belief in Jesus Christ. He then dropped me off, after asking for my business card.

In the bleak Pittsburgh train terminal, under the glow of neon lights, I watched as Amish families took their seats, eagerly awaiting the arrival of *The Pennsylvanian.*

3

A Place of Retreat

"Those Russian priests with their big bushy beards"—she didn't like them ... the big bushy beards put her off! "All that hair!"

—Mother Elizabeth

Ileana's life as Mother Alexandra cannot be fully understood without mention of the Community of Our Lady in Oshkosh, Wisconsin. This Roman Catholic community of monks was a favorite place of retreat for Ileana up until her death in 1991.

According to its website, the Community of Our Lady's motto, *NE PLUS ULTRA*, "speaks of a faith, hope, or ideal that extends beyond this transitory life." The website explains how the inspiration for its founding can be traced to Pope Pius XI, the same pope Ileana and her mother, Queen Marie, visited so that Ileana could sign a document promising to raise their children Catholic after her marriage to Archduke Anton. It continues:

In 1924, Pope Pius XI appealed to the Benedictines of the world as being most suited to engage in ecumenical relations with the Christian Churches of the East because these Churches were very much immersed in the culture of monasticism.

Fathers Regis, Eugene, and Augustine had been inspired both by the ideals of Pax Benedictina and Christian Unity—that all may be one—John 17:21. They left the Benedictine Confederation in order to establish a new kind of monastic community that would pursue St. Benedict's principles of prayer and work—the worship and seeking of God, as well as working for the monastery and for the needs of the Church, the People of God, and the unity of Christians in the contemporary world. Pope John XXIII by convoking Vatican Council II with his opening to the Eastern Orthodox, other Christian denominations, and the Jews animated the monks' proposed apostolate.

The Community website also explains how the three monks went to Rome for the blessing of Pope Paul VI for their plan:

At the Easter Vigil, April 13, 1968, Fr. Regis spoke to the pope, now St. Paul VI, who willingly approved and told him to seek out a bishop who would grant permission for the foundation. While in Europe, they took the opportunity to visit the Ecumenical Patriarch Athenagoras I in Istanbul. On April 3, 1968, he welcomed and embraced them as "My spiritual grandsons!" The Patriarch encouraged them to continue their prayer and work for Christian unity; this would become one of the central aims of the community they hoped to establish. It was in ancient Byzantium, later Constantinople, that the first community meeting was held. The next three meetings took place in Vaduz in the remote Alpine Principality of Liechtenstein, on May 14–16. They discussed the formation of a Charter of Principles meant to ensure the living out of their monastic calling while engaging with the diocesan clergy and laity, and fully participating in the life of the universal Church. There they agreed upon a distinctively unadorned title for the new entity—Community of Our Lady—inspired by Notre Dame in Paris, "Our Lady" in English, a title adopted by numerous churches and institutions.

Once the monastery was established, annual conferences were held discussing Christian unity, theology, religious life, and contemporary issues in Christianity. The founder of the Monastery of the Transfiguration, Princess Ileana, was also in attendance.

The monks of the community observe the Benedictine Rule and wear the same habits. Over time, the Monastery of Our Lady attracted international visitors, including Cardinal Jozef Glemp, Primate of Poland, who formally blessed the community in 1998.

Professed in the Benedictine Order in 1957, Fr. Augustine H. Serafini was an intimate friend of Ileana's who often posed in photographs with the princess whenever she came to the monastery for her annual retreat. My initial research into the community revealed a few false flags identifying the community as Anglo-Catholic. I asked Monk Serafini about this when I interviewed him by phone. He replied:

> That is a misconception. We use the Kyrie Eleison in the Mass and somehow that translated into some people thinking we were Anglicans or that we have only the Latin Mass, but we don't celebrate in Latin. We were founded at the time after Vatican II. Our community spun out of the Apostolate of Christian Unity at Saint Procopius Abbey in Lisle, Illinois. The Christian unity emphasis was disappearing from there and we wanted to continue it. We opted to find a monastery outside the Benedictine Order and under the authority of the local bishop—done with the permission of Pope Paul VI—so our diocese became Green Bay, Wisconsin. We had to leave the Benedictine Order but we are in the spirit of St. Benedict.

Fr. Serafini, who is in his eighties, spoke slowly but distinctly as he told the story of how the community started out with just three members:

> We were hoping to increase our numbers ... we had candidates come and go. We've had both good and bad experiences with candidates. For a while young men came in, interested in this project or that project, and that was not what we were about. You have to have a Novitiate, you have to have preparation, and many people don't like that. Our connection with Mother Alexandra—who was just south of us in the Anglican Diocese of Andeclock, the south end of Winnebago (prior to the founding of Transfiguration), a very Catholic-Anglican region—happened when we went to the archbishop and he suggested getting in touch with Mother Alexandra because we had initiated annual summer ecumenical conferences here. We had Anglican theologians and bishops and our own theologians—Roman—and religions of various kinds to speak here.

Fr. Serafini told me that as a priest and theologian, he became involved with the Greek Orthodox and Greek Catholic communities, although his favorite community was Ukrainian Catholic.

> My parish in Chicago was right near there and I would go there often. Chicago, you know, has a big Ukrainian community and St. Nicholas Cathedral is a fantastic, wonderful edifice. We were told about that in grammar school: "You should see Catholicism in a different rite." I was very fascinated. I continued that association during all my studies and celebrated Pascha with them every year and it was so beautiful.

I asked him about Ileana's trip to Rome and her marriage to Anton.

> There was a story about that. She told us that her duty was to marry Anton and she went through that, but in order to marry him she didn't have to become a Catholic but she had to raise her children Catholic, so she and Queen Marie were received in an audience by Pope Pius XI.

Fr. Serafini said that Ileana told him: "The pope was very stern with us because this was a matter of state … Queen Marie was a very important person in Europe." He continued:

> So they had to go together to the papal apartment; the pope wanted to be assured that she would raise her children Catholic—which she certainly did. She always did what she was supposed to do. Regarding her marriage to Anton, I think her original intention/spirit was to become a nun when she was young.

I asked about Ileana's retreats to the monastery and whether she attended Mass and possibly received Communion.

> She used to participate in Mass here but without receiving the Eucharist. That would have been alright because we did have a canonical procedure when Orthodox cannot commune in their own Church they can receive at the Roman Mass but they would not do

that—[meaning that Ileana and possibly other Orthodox persons who may have traveled with her refrained from taking Communion].

While the monk knew nothing of Ileana's relationship with the family of Tsar Nicholas II of Russia, he had a lot to say about the princess's own family:

She did mention her parents. Her brother Carol was a piece of work. He was a terrible person to his mother, the Queen; he was brutal, mean, because he would not allow Ileana and her husband to live in Romania. Queen Marie was more popular than anyone in Romania—Carol was diabolically jealous. There was even a kind of attempted murder; he attempted to murder Queen Marie. In one of her moments, Mother Alexandra told me that Carol had a gun and he was so angry at his mother he was ready to shoot her. It was a bitter relationship.

Fr. Serafini believed that Ileana was gifted with intuition and guided by the Holy Spirit:

Duty was inculcated in the family. She was very faithful to that. She was not a phony at all.

She was a very faithful Orthodox. The reason she came to the monastery was because of the ecumenical conferences. Later on she just wanted to spend a week here every summer. We have a guest house and she was there, all by herself. She'd come once every summer and then if we had a special celebration, ordination, anniversary, she'd always come.

She made a prayer rope for each of us. Her mother, Queen Marie, had a Catholic rosary, a very ornate rosary, which she gave us. Mother Alexandra was very genuine. When she spoke, she lived it. She was a true Christian. And I say a mystic person.

The relationship between Fr. Serafini and Mother Alexandra was very close. They were intimate friends. Ileana trusted the Community of Our Lady and Fr. Serafini to go over the manuscript of her books. "Regarding her books, she trusted us—she trusted our ideals completely," the monk said. His comment seemed to suggest some kind of source check having to do with theological issues or Church history.

I asked about Ileana's personality.

> She was very quiet but talkative at times. She communicated very well with people. She gave a talk at my 25th anniversary of ordination. In her own monastery, Transfiguration, she was receiving these monastery candidates from Romania and they wanted to wear pillbox hats with the veil; prior to that she had the perfect nun's habit: just part of the veil over her face and it was perfectly framed.

So-called pillbox veils are a trademark of Orthodox nuns in Romania, but pillbox hat veils also existed in the Catholic world before Vatican II.

I shared a story with Fr. Serafini about the modern Catholic Sisters of Saint Joseph who used to wear a kind of box veil before they reformed and began wearing secular dress with tiny cross lapel pins, stretch pants suits, and "hairdresser" hair reminiscent of the L'Oreal counter at Macy's. I told him:

> Several years ago, I had the privilege of talking to a modern St. Joe's nun when I went to a friend's Vesper memorial service at Rosemont College, a well-known Catholic institution for women.
>
> At the luncheon afterwards I sat beside a neatly coiffed woman whom I assumed was a college administrator or bank executive. She wore an emerald brooch, amber earrings, and a silk scarf, and I also smelled perfume. While slicing into a lamb chop, I asked the woman, "What do you do for a living?" When she told me she was a St. Joe's nun, I thought of the old nuns in my parochial school with their towering headgear and veils.

I told Fr. Serafini I looked in vain for a microscopic cross lapel pin that might indicate Sisterhood, but instead found a shiny brooch that indicated Boscov's.

"Years ago, when one walked the streets of Philadelphia, the only women wearing flowing religious garb were Catholic nuns or maybe a few Anglican or Lutheran nuns," I continued. "For years, I'd pass an Anglican nun in full traditional habit sitting in the concourse at 30th Street Station asking for donations." I did not have to tell Fr. Serafini that some Catholic religious orders had returned to the traditional habit and that "secular dress" orders like the St. Joe's nuns were experiencing a decline in membership, whereas convents where the traditional habit was worn were having huge membership booms.

Fr. Serafini said:

She never complained or asked for anything special in terms of food when she visited the monastery. She ate what was presented to her even if she was bound to fast from meat. [Orthodox fasts are strict and occur multiple times a year for long periods of time; in this way the Orthodox make no concessions to modernity.] She ate whatever came and she ate with the monks at the same table.

Fr. Serafini said he was 88 years old. "I'm seven years older than Joe Biden," he said—this interview was conducted in 2024—"and the same age as the pope [Francis] ... the pope is 11 months my junior. He was born in December and I was born in January of 1936."

Regarding Orthodoxy, the monk told me Ileana would refer to the Greeks (Greek Orthodox) as "very difficult people—that was her impression anyway."

Years ago, I walked into Philadelphia's Greek Orthodox cathedral of Saint George with a friend at Easter to show him what an Orthodox church was like. Immediately upon entering we were accosted by an old woman in a headscarf who shook her finger at me and in a scolding manner informed me that the cathedral was not Catholic. I told her I was aware of that and that I was merely showing the church to a Protestant friend. Her manner was so unfriendly and aggressive I did not revisit that cathedral for years afterwards.

As for the Russians, she was mostly disdainful:

Those Russian priests with their big bushy beards—she didn't like them ... the big bushy beards put her off! "All that hair!" she said.

But you, know, she was a good person with a good sense of humor. As for the Catholic-Orthodox schism, she was interested in Christian unity. She could not become a Catholic, she had to remain what she was—Orthodox—and what she was doing. The idea was that monasticism was "the bridge" between the two Churches … that is the idea that Pope Pius XI, who was a great scholar, knew a lot about … he knew a lot about her world and he knew that the Orthodox were part of The Church and because of that we have to be more united.

Politics, language, ethnic questions … these are all factors in separation, especially with the Egyptian Copts. I've always said that what made Muhammad so successful was because the Christians were always fighting.

Fr. Serafini said that Ileana was 5ft 7in. tall, and mentioned that she had an experience in childhood of a vision of an angel.

Indeed, in her book *The Holy Angels*, Ileana bridges the gap between eastern and western Christianity when she writes that "angels are realities" and "very active presences in the unfolding of the drama of creation and the working out of the daily life of our world."

If we ignore their presence, help, and care, "we deprive ourselves of a great source of consolation, strengthening and hope."

In the introduction to *The Holy Angels*, Eastern Catholic monk M. Basil Pennington comments that when Ileana writes about the monastic tradition, she does not stick to her own tradition (Orthodoxy) but goes beyond the dividing line of the Great Schism when she calls Bernard of Clairvaux a "great Cistercian mystic" who elaborated on the teachings of the fifth-century Syrian monk known as Pseudo-Dionysius and by doing so incorporated those teachings into the Western tradition. Fr. Serafini said:

She was very close to the angelic world, and the saints were very important to her. She followed Christ so closely: she suffered, repented, was humble and the Kingdom of God for her was first.

He talked about her compassion when one of the three priests at his monastery became very ill and she nursed him back to health. Yet this was no superficial Hallmark Card compassion. "She was compatible with everybody—the Anglican priests' wives, Catholic,

Orthodox ... She always had a gift when she came here like a metal icon or a triptych."

The ecumenical spirit evident in Ileana's life had its counterpart in Fr. Serafini's world. He grew up in a small family in the 1930s and began studying for the priesthood in Chicago when he entered an Archdiocesan high school for pre-seminary students. "I was an only child for a long time, and that was enjoyable, but being the elder brother is not an enviable position."

His childhood parish was close to the jurisdiction of Archbishop Iakovos, the Greek Orthodox Metropolitan in Chicago and Primate of the Greek Orthodox Archdiocese of North and South America between 1959 and 1996. Fr. Serafini recalled:

> His jurisdiction came up to Wisconsin. Our monastery was very close to him. He was congenial and very ecumenical and we were very close to him. I had dealings with a Greek real estate agent in Chicago once and I asked him if he was from Assumption (GO [Greek Orthodox]) parish in Chicago, and he said "Oh yes," and then I asked him if he knew a particular priest there and he says, "Oh that man ... we're going to get rid of him because he's pushing frequent communion."

Frequent communion in Orthodoxy used to be frowned upon, although that is rarely the case today. "I had read that the ban on frequent communion had a basis in the Jansenist heresy and ideology that had infected the Orthodox Church," Fr. Serafini said.

We discussed other Catholic-Orthodox differences, such as fasting. There are some variations in fasting in the Orthodox Church depending on jurisdictions, but Orthodox Christians generally fast anywhere from 180 to 200 days per year. The faithful are advised to avoid olive oil, meat, fish, wine, and dairy. Before taking the Eucharist, abstinence from food and drink after midnight preceding the Divine Liturgy is the rule, although some exceptions may exist if one has the blessing of a bishop. The Roman Church, on the other hand, has all but eliminated fasting.

"Regarding fasting, we went to the other extreme in the Roman Church," Father Serafini added. He recalled the time immediately following his ordination when all the changes from Vatican II were being implemented: "When these changes were happening, it was kind of embarrassing because I had to explain these things that were happening to the people in the church at the Mass."

Although he described himself as "a campaigner" for the vernacular in the Roman rite since he was in high school, when the time came for the promulgation of the new Mass and when the liturgy professor was announcing what was going to happen, Fr. Serafini admitted he "got scared."

> I was really upset because the new Mass was such a departure. Those who came into the Roman Church as a body—the Anglicans—they have a beautiful English Mass; that's what I envisioned what we would have. It was so simple; all the chants are in English and so forth ... But the great minds of France, Belgium, Netherlands, and Germany had other ideas.
>
> They went back to basically early Christian times, early Medieval—say if you were in St. Augustine's diocese in North Africa, the Mass would be something like that.

To bring back a sense of mystery and majesty in the liturgy, Fr. Serafini said he would celebrate in the Catholic Slavonic Rite.

> I don't do that anymore because Mother Alexandra mentioned that the Orthodox don't like it. She said: "We don't like the idea of Latin Catholics putting on the other vestments and celebrating in the Byzantine Rite." She said that was a kind of phony thing unless you have to staff a parish where you have Maronites or Melkites and you need a priest. At that point it would be a good reason to celebrate in another rite ...
>
> Anyway, I love the Ukrainians. The Ukrainians sang like angels; their liturgy was just tremendous. You know, I have this opinion that women were not destined to sing in church. Women were forbidden to be in the choir in the Medieval Church.

4

The Mother Elizabeth Connection

Diversion. Distraction. Fantasy. Change of fashion, food, love and landscape. We need them as the air we breathe. Without change our brains and bodies rot.

—Bruce Chatwin

When I requested a press review copy of *I Live Again*, I was on a reading trajectory that included Archbishop Chrysostomos's *A Greek Orthodox Nun in Buckingham Palace* as well as a rare (and out of print) book entitled *The 6,000 Beards of Athos* by Ralph H. Brewster.

Author Ralph H. Brewster's grandfather was the celebrated German sculptor, Adolf Hildebrand (1847–1921), said to be the most important German sculptor between 1880 and the end of World War One. Adolf's son, Dietrich von Hildebrand (1889--1977), was a Roman Catholic philosopher and religious writer whom Pope Pius XII referred to as a "Doctor of the Church." Dietrich's wife, the Belgian-born Alice von Hildebrand (1923–2022), was also a Catholic philosopher and theologian, the author of many books, including *The Soul of a Lion*, about her husband. She also wrote for the intellectual conservative Catholic magazine, *New Oxford Review*. Brewster was one of three sons born to Adolf's daughter, Elizabeth.

The 6,000 Beards of Athos was considered scandalous and controversial when it was first published by Leonard and Virginia Woolf in 1935. The book dealt with the personal lives of monks on the holy mountain of Mount Athos in Greece. It went against conventional assumptions about what a monk's life should be. In the Prologue to the book, Brewster writes:

"But of course there are women on Mount Athos! How would it be possible for six thousand men to live together without a single woman? I visited the monastery of Lavra last year, and I am sure that the under-secretary, at any rate, is a woman disguised as a monk. I made a photograph of him: there can hardly be any doubt. You have only to look at his face—her face."

This statement, made by the Italian archeologist, Dr. L-------, was for me the final touch. I could restrain my curiosity about the Holy Mountain no longer. I felt I must go there and penetrate its mystery ...

Were there women on Mount Athos? Or was this only the imagination of an Italian to whom the idea of a land without women was a natural impossibility? At any rate, this had not been suggested to me before. But then everything I heard about Athos was so contradictory! No two people who spoke to me about it ever said the same thing.

Later in the book, Brewster tells the story of Lorgos and Lucian, two young monks at the idiorrhythmic monastery of Vatopedi:

...Lorgos and Lucian had disappeared together across the fields, and were lying side by side among the vines. The older monks noticed the incident and whispered comments to each other. Lucian was just 19, and had only been a year at Vatopedi. He once came on a visit, and, liking the life so much, decided to become a monk. He said he adored girls, and really became a monk because girls like monks. He seemed to think he would have far greater success now, than if he were a layman. He dreamt of having a virgin, he said; but he could hardly expect to find one at Vatopedi after all!

Several hours later, when the two young monks are in the "charming apartment" of Father Sophronios, the two sat together on a couch when Lorgos began stroking Lucian's face. The rest I will leave to the reader's imagination.

Of course, when many contemporary literate people think of Mount Athos they may think of the English travel writer, Bruce Chatwin.

* * *

My interest in Princess Ileana and her world legacy had its roots in social media.

Early in 2024, Mother Elizabeth (Carol Klipa Bacha) of the New Tikhvin Skete of the Holy Mother of God in Palm Coast, Florida, sent me a Facebook message, long after I had read most of Ileana's memoir and then put it back on the shelf, thinking "What possible interest can this book hold for me?" I'd accepted Mother Elizabeth's "friend" request on Facebook because I was intrigued at her status as an Orthodox nun. Priests and other male clergy are generally more prone to reaching out like this, while nuns tend to be anchored to a more private life. Then again, perhaps Mother Elizabeth (or "M.E.") was responding to my posted Facebook essays on Catholicism and Orthodoxy and felt that we had shared interests.

When M.E. asked that I give her a call, I knew something unusual was up. No sooner had we connected than she began talking about Mother Alexandra:

> I met Mother Alexandra in 1974 at the Orthodox Christian Fellowship (OCF) gathering of college-aged students. OCF was very strong at the time. This was a pan-Orthodox meeting in Pittsburgh but I didn't go there planning on meeting Mother Alexandra, but when I did she invited me to the monastery in Ellwood City. I had come up from Florida because I was on a mission for Christ the Savior Church there—which later became a cathedral—and working for Fr. George A. Gladky (1931–1989), who I didn't know at the time was my blood father. With his help we moved up boxes of books, icons and I carried crosses that we made in Miami for the conference, and I set the whole thing up in one of the hotel rooms. The hotel room became a kind of bookstore and Mother Alexandra came into that room. In those days, books about Orthodoxy were very limited but I had a very diverse selection.

The two kept in touch after that, but then in 1989, when M.E. applied for the position of youth coordinator for the Orthodox Church of America (OCA), she asked Mother Alexandra to write a recommendation. Mother Alexandra not only wrote a recommendation, but recounted her experience of meeting Carol Bacha in Pittsburgh, while acknowledging that young Carol not only knew about the books at the OCF conference but knew what was in them.

"So this was my introduction to the invitation I eventually received to visit the monastery," M.E. recalled. "This was my bond with Mother Alexandra: books."

Educated at Indiana University in Indiana, Pennsylvania, where she also worked in the music library and studied Russian, Bacha thought she was on her way to Alaska to do missionary work when a combination of factors—orchestrated partly by Fr. George Gladky, whom she would later discover was actually her biological father—brought her to Ellwood City, where Ileana was busy building the Monastery of the Transfiguration.

Bacha said that there were two nuns with Ileana at the time, one of them "a Sister Catherine, who was my age." These visits were cut short because Fr. Gladky kept calling her back to Miami. "Every time I would go to the monastery he would find an excuse to get me back. He'd say things like: 'We need you to do this.'" (At the time, Fr. Gladky knew Bacha was his daughter, which may explain his insistence that she always return to Florida.)

It was not long before Bacha became Ileana's assistant and confidante.

It wasn't easy for Mother Alexandra to write a book because she didn't have a high school education let alone a degree or academic pedigree so that a publisher would easily pick her up or print her books as a nun.

Bacha of course was referring to books like *I Live Again* and *The Holy Angels*. She continued:

She had a fantastic tutor's education growing up in England in Queen Victoria's Court. But it was interrupted by the war. Basil Pennington was the one who made *The Holy Angels* book possible because nobody else would pick it up. He took over where I left off and got it printed and published. I helped her review the whole manuscript because she didn't graduate from high school. I would spell check for her. She would say things like, "Ellwood City should just be spelled with one 'l', why do you have two? You will find in copies of her letters she would spell Ellwood with only one 'l'."

Bacha says that Ileana was very particular with her choice of words:

I didn't really help her as an editor would; I was mainly a workhorse of typing and spell check. All of the chapters of the *Angels* book were published in one form or another by the magazine that the Romanian Episcopate put out. But she didn't write them sitting in an office. We didn't have Google then. She did this research when she would travel back to her monastery in France and then go visit her children in Europe and Salzburg where Mozart lived. She would go to the library and do this research. This was our bond, because here I am the library person, but the entire thing was very much like a war between a protagonist and antagonist at Transfiguration, mainly because Sister Catherine didn't want any of that [activities related to the book].

When I first went to the Ellwood monastery it was very difficult because I came in sort of like her soul mate. Sister Catherine at that time was only a postulant; she had her own problems. She more or less terrorized the entire monastery so eventually the acting superior, Mother Benedicta, got rid of her. Sister Catherine was just limited because she came from a little village in northern Pennsylvania, whereas Mother Alexandra—Ileana—was multi-continental.

I was taken aback at Bacha's depiction of one of the earliest nuns at Transfiguration as "terrorizing" the monastery. Terror can take many forms, however. They say "The Church" is a hospital for sinners, but the same thing can be said about monasteries. She added:

I had grown up all my life as an Orthodox Christian and was a missionary in Miami, whereas Sister Catherine was a convert and she thought that the running of monasteries should be done according to the book.

Bacha then went on to describe how she helped Ileana type up the letters that she sent to Metropolitan Anthony Bloom, Ileana's spiritual father.

Anthony Bloom (Metropolitan Anthony of Sourozh, 1914–2003) was the son of a Russian diplomat who survived the October Revolution but lived abroad. An atheist in his youth, a still-young Bloom converted to Christianity and was ordained a priest in 1948. He was later consecrated a bishop, then made Archbishop-Metropolitan for Great Britain and Ireland.

The Filosofia: An Encyclopedia of Russian Thought, describes Bloom as follows:

Of all major Orthodox thinkers, Anthony of Sourozh places the least emphasis on Church tradition, focusing instead on the complexities of the personal encounter between man and God. His theology is anthropologically oriented toward the existential circumstances of modernity: the psychological anxieties of contemporary humanity, its feelings of alienation, loneliness, and obsession with materialistic pursuits. Anthony does not seek to refute materialism from some "super-spiritual" or purely idealistic point of view, but argues, rather, that Christianity serves the glorification of the material world better than does atheistic materialism. "Christianity is the only perfect materialism in the sense that a materialist regards matter as a constructing material, whereas for us matter acquires an absolute significance; it is sacred because of the embodiment of Christ, in Whom the fullness of Divinity dwelled corporeally."

"Mother Alexandra used the book [*Holy Angels*] to protect me," Bacha continued. "By that I mean she wanted to keep me at her monastery."

Nuns are supposed to have some form of work that they do during the day. She made this a part of my work so she could call me to her cell and tell me this family history and prepare me to be the abbess. She gave me everything I needed to do to be abbess. She gave me drawings of what the monastery needed to look like as it grew. She told me about her formation and how it came about. We were like ... well, I had more of a college roommate connection with her than I had when I was in Indiana with a college roommate.

Sister Catherine, who was really just a kid without a lot of experience, didn't like it when historians came around and wanted to interview Mother Alexandra about being a princess in Romania. She thought that was out of place for the monastery. And Mother Alexandra herself said that people in general weren't allowed to come and talk to the nuns about their history and things like that. That was a kind of rule but she broke that rule in a sense with me to intimately share every picture book that was at that time in the library and common room and tell me her life story and entrust me with these special things.

Bacha talked about a priest-monk who later became a bishop who played the part of the antagonist in the early part of Mother Alexandra's story:

He supported Sister Catherine's war against Mother Alexandra under her own roof. The priest was an aspiring bishop who used Sister Catherine to undermine the monastic authority of Mother Alexandra. He did this while Mother Alexandra was away on a trip for six weeks. He told Sister Catherine that she could now use the Jerusalem Bible for the psalms reading in the chapel. Now, Mother Alexandra didn't permit that because the thing was we worked on the prayer book—the whole life of the monastery was from the King James Bible ... that's what Mother Alexandra knew by heart. The initial people who helped her with the monastery were the Episcopal Women of the Prayer Book Society. The Orthodox wouldn't have anything to do with Mother Alexandra initially.

The bishop that she tried to be under before she went with the Romanians in 1970 when the Orthodox Church in America became the OCA, was Bishop Athanasuis, but he left for Holy Trinity Monastery in Jordanville, New York. The OCA wouldn't be the OCA today if it wasn't for Mother Alexandra. She was that pan-Orthodox and she was going to work to make sure that America embraced pan-Orthodoxy.

In other words, she would give the U.S. a vision or working model of Christian Orthodoxy that was not so ethnic. That would be Mother Alexandra's mission.

Bacha believed that the books about Mother Alexandra's life have been whitewashed clean:

> It's whitewashed that Mother Benedicta was kicked out of a monastery in Michigan. The books don't say that she was kicked out and that she came to Florida and because of my history with Mother Alexandra she was trying to help me and her start a monastery in Florida.

Bacha is right regarding the whitewashing of Mother Benedicta's history. Certainly there's no mention of this in the literature at the Monastery of the Transfiguration. After all, Mother Benedicta served as abbess of Transfiguration from 1978 to 1986, so what purpose would this information serve other than we are all human, even those of us who may aspire to become saints?

Expulsion from a monastery may happen for a number of reasons.

In the Western Church, there is St. Benedict Joseph Labre, born in 1748, who was a saint set apart because he was rejected by multiple monasteries but ultimately chose the life of a holy wanderer—called a Holy Fool in the Eastern Church. He never bathed and stunk so badly even his confessor insisted that they not meet in the confinement of a confessional. The saint's famous saying is: "I shall not remain in the world." He has been adopted as the patron saint of people with autism, mental illness, and those experiencing homelessness. A statue of St. Benedict Joseph Labre can be found in the Catholic National Shrine of the Immaculate Conception in Washington, D.C.

Mother Benedicta's brother, Archimandrite Roman Braga, is up for canonization in the Romanian Orthodox Church. Father Roman suffered the unimaginable cruelty of Romanian communist prisons, most notably solitary confinement, after the communists abolished the monarchy, the cause of Princess Ileana's exile to the United States. Mother Elizabeth says that Fr. Roman paved the way for her during her years of "persona non gratis" when she was studying to get her music degree and to get a roof over her head.

Princess Ileana of Romania as a small girl, *c.* 1910. (*Library of Congress*)

Princess Ileana, *c.* 1920.
(*Bibliothèque nationale de France*)

Above left and above right: Tsarevich Alexei Nikolaevich and Princess Ileana aboard the *Standart*, the imperial Russian yacht. Alexei was the youngest child and only son of Tsar Nicholas II and Tsarina Alexandra Feodorovna. His four sisters were Olga, Tatiana, Maria, and Anastasia. He inherited the "royal disease" of hemophilia. Though doted upon heavily and even spoiled as a child, his hemophilia caused him great suffering. He once said to his mother, "When I'm dead, it won't hurt anymore, will it?" Alexei was a great reader and loved people to read to him aloud. (*Library of Congress*)

Tsar Nicholas II with Tsarevich Alexei. Because of his hemophilia, the tsar and tsarina believed Alexei would not survive to become tsar. According to Carol Bacha (Mother Elizabeth), Princess Ileana's (Mother Alexandra's) assistant for several years, a secret rendezvous was arranged between Nicholas II and Queen Marie of Romania at the marriage of Grand Duchess Maria Pavlovna of Russia and Prince Vilhelm of Sweden in 1908 to ensure a healthy male heir to the Russian throne. The result of that union was the birth of Princess Ileana. (*Stock, Science Source*)

The so-called Mad Monk of Russia, Grigori Rasputin, had healing and clairvoyant abilities. The Serbian-born mystic was known to have healed Tsarevich Alexei on multiple occasions. The tsarevich wore a locket around his neck with Rasputin's photo inside. Here Rasputin is shown blessing an unknown person. Rasputin scholars like Douglas Smith concur that no Orthodox priest would have thought to adopt such a pose for a photographer. (*Library of Congress*)

Queen Marie, Princess Ileana, and her brother Nicholas arriving in New York City in 1926 aboard the *Leviathan*. (*Stock*)

Princess Ileana's mother, Queen Marie of Romania. (*Library of Congress*)

Princess Ileana posing in
traditional Romanian dress,
c. 1925. (*Library of Congress*)

Above: Princess Ileana of Romania, the Earl of Luton, the Crown Prince of Abyssinia, Alfonso XIII, and his wife, Princess Victoria Eugenie of Battenberg. The AP reported in 1924 that Princess Ileana was going to Madrid to arrange her wedding. There were reports of an engagement between Ileana and King Alfonso XIII's eldest son, the Prince of Asturias. Queen Marie reportedly did not support the union, and the romance between the prince and Ileana did not last. (*Stock*)

Left: Princess Ileana wearing a Spanish dress. It was on her first visit to Spain in 1930 that Ileana met Archduke Anton of Austria, whom she married the following year. (*Stock/Historical Findings*)

Above: Bran Castle, Transylvania. Mother Alexander (Princess Ileana) was against "the Dracula-ization" of her castle. Vlad the Impaler (Dracula) never lived at or even visited the castle. (*Library of Congress*)

Right: The Holy Trinity Church, Cozia Monastery, established by Volvode (Prince) Mircea I of Wallachia. (*The author*)

Princess Ileana (Mother Alexandra) fell in love with the western Pennsylvania countryside because it reminded her of Transylvania. This wide-field view of the Monastery of the Transfiguration is the kind of landscape she wanted. (*The author*)

Above left: Mother Alexandra (Ileana) at the Monastery of the Transfiguration in Ellwood City, Pennsylvania, a monastery for women she founded in 1967. (*Monastery of the Transfiguration*)

Above right: The author with Abbess Gabriela Platon of Voroneţ Monastery, or the Sistine Chapel of the East. Built by Stephen the Great (now a saint in the Romanian Orthodox Church) in 1488, the monastery's blue color is now referred to by artists as "Voronet blue." The monastery is a UNESCO Heritage site in Bucovina, famous for its fresco of The Last Judgment. (*The author*)

These were difficult years, she said, as the money in her college stipend was running out. She had also recently divorced her Orthodox priest husband, Teddy, because he left her and the family and the priesthood all at once. Fearing she would not have a roof over her head, Fr. Roman helped to support her financially—he had come to Ellwood City in 1978—and wanted M.E. to remain at Transfiguration.

After her divorce, Bacha was tonsured a nun in 2015:

I always thought that Fr. Roman would tonsure me a nun. He told me what to do: at the time I was involved with ROCOR [Russian Orthodox Church Outside of Russia] in Palm Coast, where I bought my house. He stated that he should be my bishop, so he blessed everything on the Sunday of the Cross in Great Lent, 2015, then he passed away to Great Eternity on Bright Tuesday, 2015.

Carol Bacha was born in Steelton, Pennsylvania, a suburb of Harrisburg. She grew up in a third-floor apartment down from the local fire station. "I rode fire trucks before I was five years old, and my mother dated the fire chief. My dad never traveled anywhere in his life except within a 15-mile radius; that's why he wouldn't let me go to Alaska with eight women missionaries in the fall of 1972."

Talk of marriage and divorce led us back to Ileana and her second marriage after her divorce from Prince Anton of Austria:

She wanted to be a nun when she married him; it was a marriage of convenience to get her safely to America, though she did try to make it a real marriage. And he [Ileana's new husband] tried to do with her what people tried to do with me before I became a nun: they tried to use me to sell Russian-speaking women to be a dating service. Because I was a high-profile figure for a dating service as Mother Alexandra's long-time assistant—they wanted me. The situation then parallels what is happening today. This is why I don't go to the ROCOR Church in my own country. They don't want me anyway because I don't agree to their agenda, which is gold digging.

"There are gold-digging dating services sponsored by Orthodox Christians?" I asked, somewhat shocked.

Yes. There's more people that I met that went there [the dating service] at one time that don't go there anymore because their agenda has just been to sell people and make money off the marriage that usually happens soon after. I don't know how many other parishes do that in ROCOR, but you know there is not much difference between that and human trafficking."

Mother Elizabeth added:

The service is protected because some of the women sold were sent to the Flagler County Sheriff. They bought me a house in Orlando that I lived in for about ten years. I thought this house was going to be our monastery; they helped me go to Russia. They showed me the plight of the women there—they weren't ROCOR when they tried to sell me, they were still OCA, the same group out of Orlando City. The ROCOR church where I am, well, they are not interested in building a church or chapel like I want to do because they have this rental situation where they can control the money, and who comes in and who goes out, and then they get rid of the intermediary ... just like you would sell Tupperware. They try to mould these women into sellable forces.

Bacha directed me to the Orlando St. Nicholas Church Facebook page, and then she came down with the most horrible charge of all: "They use Confession because they secretly photograph the women going to Confession so you can see who you will get." Meaning of course the buyer will see who he gets after inspecting the women in the photograph.

I asked her if the situation with Florida ROCOR was happening in parishes across the United States.

I don't know. It might be happening in your own town and you don't even see it. I was talking with the chancellor for the Romanian Episcopate for the OCA, and we talked about it and we were both in agreement against it, but we both agreed that the practice has become normalized.

My doctor and I just discussed this situation recently. Apparently there are thousands and thousands of them, men and women in Europe, in this situation right now. And some of them when they get married, the marriages last about a year to two years ... there's no real family life in these marriages, no real counseling.

I asked Bacha again how any Orthodox priest could align himself with arrangements regarding the sale of women.

Because the priest in question didn't go to seminary and he got set up by another priest, and this priest didn't go to seminary either but had a biological father who was a priest, and they have money and they control the eastern ROCOR, and this is what they do. They don't care how long this war goes on because it is all about money in their pockets.

Bacha spoke about "red light/green light" attempts to correct the situation, all failures, because this is what is happening in ROCOR right now.

They really screwed up in Miami: the oldest Orthodox church in Miami—Saints Peter and Paul—is empty, vacant, because they had a ROCOR deacon there that they didn't screen. And they found out later that he had a criminal background. They don't screen people!

5

Dating Services and Tainted Love

Mother Elizabeth spared no words:

You can go online to see that in Orlando there's a dating service called Prestige Dating Service. When I was attending the rental church of the ROCOR in Dayton, Florida, the lady that runs the Prestige Dating Service would come out with a camera and lens 8 inches long and take pictures that she could use in the selling of women. They had it so people could come from any state and just drop in and get married or even baptized, and not be part of the community again. That priest in Dayton has since gone over to the Greeks—an organization that sells women.

Orthodox priests not attending or graduating from seminaries occurs in Orthodoxy, whereas seminary training is a requirement in the Roman Catholic Church. In my own life I have met and worked with Orthodox priests who were ordained because their fathers were priests or because they were already tonsured readers or sub-deacons and the bishop felt that the shortage of priests made their ordination necessary. I have also witnessed certain loopholes taken advantage of when it comes to the ordination of deacons. In one case, a certain deacon was divorced and then remarried a divorced woman, but he was ordained a deacon anyway because the pastor of a parish desperately needed an assistant, something that clearly goes against the canons of the Russian Orthodox Church.

Loopholes taken in the name of clergy shortages are certainly questionable, although in the early Church the idea of a seminary was completely foreign.

As (the now deceased) Ihumen Gregory Woolfenden wrote in *The Ukrainian Orthodox World*:

> In the history of the Orthodox Church, seminaries as we know them today are a relatively recent invention. In fact, nothing like modern seminaries existed anywhere before the sixteenth century.
>
> In the early days of the Church it was not unusual for people to be simply chosen out of the community for whatever ministry it was felt they should exercise. St. Ambrose of Milan (Fourth Century) was not even baptized when chosen by acclamation to be Bishop of the city. The lives of the saints are full of stories of how men tried to avoid ordination, St. John Chrysostom being a very good example, fleeing to the hilly wilderness around Antioch in order to avoid being made a priest. We still have a relic of those days in our service of ordination, a deacon who is to be ordained priest is brought to the altar by a deacon and handed over to two priests who conduct him around the altar. Originally this was to stop him running away!

On the other hand, Ihumen Gregory writes that there has been a huge revival of seminaries in Russia, Ukraine, and Belarus:

> They are gaining state validation once more and they have numerous students, but are often critically short of well-trained staff. An interesting development in Moscow has been the St Tikhon's Theological Institute. This very large and well staffed institution has mainly concentrated on lay training in Theology and related subjects. However, many of their formerly part-time students have been ordained on the strength of this training. These are often older men who have had another career and are in many cases proving to be excellent, educated and spiritual priests.

* * *

When Ileana married Dr. Stefan Nikolaus Issarescu, a Romanian pathologist, in 1954 after her divorce from Anton, she faced the "selling market" that Bacha talked about. Bacha claimed

Dr. Issarescu tried to use Ileana to make the Prestige Dating Service in Orlando "prestigious." Bacha and others also claim the marriage was one of convenience: to get Ileana and her children out of Romania safely.

A *New York Times* article from 1954 describes the second marriage of Illeana to Issarescu in his Newton, Massachusetts home. (Ileana and the pathologist would divorce in 1965.)

> NEWTON, Mass., June 19— Princess Ileana of Rumania and Dr. Stefan Issarescu were married here at noon in a ceremony at the home of the bride. The Rev. Nicholas Vanuch of the Syrian Orthodox Church in Boston officiated. Princess Ileana has been living here with her six children since 1948. She divorced her first husband, Archduke Anton of Austria, several years ago. Dr. Issarescu was born in Rumania. He received a Doctor of Laws degree at the University of Bucharest and studied medicine at Charles University in Prague, Czechoslovakia. During World War II, he spent some time in concentration camps and later worked for a refugee organization transporting displaced persons.

Little in the current "Ileana literature" is given over to the princess's engagement to Count Alexander von Hochberg, a German aristocrat and military officer, perhaps the one true love of her life.

Born in 1905 to Hans Heinrich XV, 3rd Prince von Pless, and his wife Daisy, Princess of Pless, Alexander officially became a Polish citizen after the nation's annexation of parts of Germany. On January 30, 1930, he and Princess Ileana announced their engagement.

The blog *Royal Musings*, for the date January 30, 1930, states:

> Princess Ileana beamed as she spoke with a reporter at a dinner given in her honor at Predeal by the Romanian Gymnastics Institute. The Princess is the patron of the organization.
>
> "I'm marrying for love only," she said, as her fiancé Count Alexander von Hochberg, stood beside her. She described their relationship as a "happy love match."
>
> *The New York Times* reports that after the princess' adjutant Colonel Manolescu formally announced her engagement to Count Alexander, there was "loud and prolonged cheering."

The President of the Gymnastics Institute expressed hope that Ileana would not desert her country; the Princess, showing signs of being visually touched by the support for her engagement.

Count Alexander said he promised to spend "the greater part of the year" in Romania and he and his wife would be "abroad for only a few months."

The Romanian Court officially announced Princess Ileana's engagement this morning. The formal betrothal, which is popular throughout the country, took place earlier today at Cotrocenci Palace. The entire royal family was present including the three regents for the young King Michael and military and government officials, as well as Prime Minister Julius Maniu.

The wedding will take place at Sinaia on April 27. Count Alexander will return to London to visit his family. His mother, Princess Daisy, is one of Queen Marie's closest friends.

The Princess, who was dressed in a Romanian national costume and her fiancé stayed until the end of dinner. Afterward she changed into an evening dress and she and her fiancé left for a night out at the Sinaia Casino, where they danced until 4 o'clock in the morning.

The Queen and her daughter are planning to travel to Syria, Palestine and Egypt during February and will return to Romania together.

Count Alexander, who is 25 years old, is the second son of the prince of Pless. He and Ileana have been together for several months.

The marriage never took place, however, because the Romanian government discovered that Alexander—or Lexel—had been involved in a homosexual relationship. The truth was revealed when news of the engagement caused the police to turn over an official report to the government.

TIME magazine reported the end of the engagement on March 17, 1930:

Some twenty days of hard work by the Rumanian Foreign Office ended last week when effeminate Count Alexander ("Lexel") von Hochberg, descendant of the ancient and glorious Piast Kings of

Poland, son of the German Prince of Pless, at last—in the words of the official Rumanian communique—"consented to permit the breaking of his engagement with H. R. H. Princess Ileana of Rumania."

Bucharest papers confidently asserted that Dowager Queen Marie, who was houseboating on the Nile with Princess Ileana last week, had persuaded her daughter, who is of age and has a private fortune of $260,000, that she must not marry the Count.

If it has done nothing else the Ileana-Alexander faux pas has boosted the sale of Alexander's mother's book: *Daisy, Princess of Pless, by Herself* (Button, $5). Through its 529 pages prurient persons are searching feverishly for an allusion to the Count's effeminate practices, cause of the matchruptcy. Shrewd, the Button sales department led them in as deep as possible last week with this brand new blurb:

"He was a sensitive lad, for while his mother was writing these memoirs he reminded her of the repugnance he felt at the age of 15 toward a practise he then encountered in his uncle's country house in Silesia.

"The establishment was maintained on very old fashioned lines. Ugly blue-glass finger bowls, with a blue-glass tumbler inside them containing the necessary mixture, were placed in front of each guest and at the end of each meal, conscientiously and noisily used. After this revolting gargling, the party entered the drawing room and, before coffee was served, all the relations gave each other a resounding kiss, at the same time saying, Mahlzeit, meaning good digestion.

"Lexel adds that, horrid as the gargling in the dining room was, it at least served to mitigate the beastliness of being kissed by a lot of people whose mouths and beards smelled and tasted of dinner! But then Lexel never did like promiscuous embraces, and, as a very small boy, once flatly refused to kiss even the Emperor's hand!

"But when the houseboat *Mayflower* left Aswan, last week, keen eyed Egyptians saw that the solitaire diamond Princess Ileana accepted from 'Lexel' still twinkled on H.R.H.'s engagement finger."

* * *

Mother Alexandra's soul mate and the survival of Russian royalty

"I became Mother Alexandra's soul mate in many ways," Bacha says. "Now, according to the historian Harry Binkow, there are numerous people that knew the Bolshevik murder of the family of the tsar didn't happen. Composer Sergei Rachmaninoff was one of these people."

Bacha had made many references to the survival of the tsar's family. She would continue to send me documents and news stories related to this story, most especially information about historian Harry Binkow. The "guts" of this story will be addressed later in the book, but as a teaser Bacha sent me this letter from Binkow to the CIA which was approved for release (as the letter states) in 2021.

Approved for Release: 2021/11/10 CO5571705 W, Central Intelligence Agency
Office of Public Afiairs
Washington, DC. 20505
703-613-3607
Freedom of Information Act inquiry.

RE: A Romanov File

I am a Historian Investigator, writing a book about the Imperial Family of Russia. There have been many stories written about their possible rescue, and that there is a file formally identified as, "The Chiver's Papers." The Soviet Union, in 1977, was aware, that these documents were to be declassified. In July 1977, the former Impatiev House, in Ekaterinburg, was leveled, to further eliminate any evidence for research. The Documents on file should be that of foreign archives, that indicate the Imperial Family did not die, but survived and continued their living in other countries. This is all that I have read, regarding this subject. I am writing to determine whether these documents have been declassified.

Best regards,
Harry M. Binkow

Bacha had been in communication with Binkow up until the latter's death from AIDS in 1993. According to Bacha and Binkow, the tsar's family were secretly escorted from Ekaterinburg—the place where history tells us they were executed—to different parts of Europe. Bacha told me that Alexei changed his name, migrated to the United States, married, and worked for the United Nations; he is buried near the Serbian Orthodox cathedral in Belgrade. To confirm Alexei's survival, Bacha sent me a newspaper interview with the tsar's son conducted in the 1960s. The published interview explains (see Appendix) in detail what happened to the family after their supposed executions.

For now, what was uppermost on Bacha's mind was what she considered to be a major ROCOR scandal:

When they (ROCOR) helped me go to Russia for a visit I didn't know that I was getting into their program of trying to sell women. This is what they were doing at Valaam—not the monks—but they had a group that would organize honeymoons after these sales—a river cruise that would go to Valaam where they would dance and had state rooms where people could meet and buy each other and then stay at Valaam. (The Valaam Monastery is a stauropegic Orthodox monastery in Russian Karelia established in the tenth century by a Greek monk, Sergia of Valaam.)

The house that ROCOR got for me was $350,000. They handled the mortgage. They said the house could be used as a monastery. Then they brought me a woman that I was supposed to sell. This was an OCA parish that went ROCOR. In ROCOR there are a few priests in the eastern diocese who get a regular salary, so the selling of women is a source of income. It's a gold-digger thing for these parishes. They have normalized this rather than give the priests a salary.

She added:

But, you know, 200 years ago all the old-world parish priests got was a chicken. But the ROCOR priests make anywhere from $3,000 to $6,000 when they baptize the women or men involved in the selling, and then marry them. Today, the OCA wants to adopt this system as do the Greeks. They all want in on it.

The conversation then switched to Queen Marie's relationship with Illeana. Ileana, she said, was able to tell her stories about her mother, Queen Marie, who had a love for literature, was an avid reader, a poet, writer, and artist. The queen's drawings were exhibited in Paris and London. She also wrote several novels. Her striking blue eyes were noted by almost everyone who met her. Marie, who was born into the British royal family to Prince Alfred, Duke of Edinburgh, and Grand Duchess Maria Alexandrovna—the daughter of Tsar Alexander II of Russia—was the last queen of Romania (she was queen from October 10, 1914 to July 1927). Prince George of Wales courted Marie and proposed marriage, but because they were first cousins and the Russian Orthodox Church forbade first-cousin marriages, Marie declined the proposal. The Duchess of Edinburgh, Marie's mother, did not want her daughter to stay in England, so a marriage was proposed by King Carol of Romania, who wanted to ensure succession to Crown Prince Ferdinand. After an engagement was announced, Ferdinand gave Marie money to purchase jewelry.

Marie was Anglican (she was received into the Romanian Orthodox Church in 1926), while Ferdinand was Catholic, so the couple had three wedding ceremonies, one in each of their respective religions and one civil ceremony. Queen Marie devoted much of her time during World War One giving away provisions and rehabilitating and nursing Romanian soldiers while traveling around the country in the royal Rolls Royce.

Known as the Queen Mother of the Balkans, historians agree that Prince Barbu Alexandru, the thirtieth prime minister of Romania in 1927 and with whom she had an affair, was the father of Queen Marie's youngest son, Mircea, and quite possibly Ileana herself.

In 1926, Queen Marie—hailed as "the most beautiful and the popular ruler in all of Europe"—her son Nicholas and Ileana, then aged 17, sailed across the Atlantic and embarked on a train trip across North America. The journey comprised some 10,087 miles. They left on the SS *Leviathan* on the evening of October 12, 1926, and arrived in New York, where they were greeted by a ticker-tape parade on October 18. After visiting Niagara Falls and Washington, D.C., where they dined with President Coolidge, they boarded a luxury train, *The Royal Roumanian*, which closely followed the Northwest Passage Trail first explored by Lewis and Clark between 1803 and 1806. In North Dakota, where they attended a rodeo, Queen Marie was named a "Sister of the Sioux" by the Sioux Indian tribe. The train took them through Colorado and Washington State, where they visited a lumber camp, and then went over the Cascade Mountains in Canada.

The royals had planned to visit the American South as well, but Queen Marie decided to cut the trip short in mid-November when she learned that the health of her husband, King Ferdinand, was failing. They sailed out of New York and back to Europe aboard the RMS *Berengaria* on November 24.

Bacha said:

The trip was really Ileana's introduction to America. In a physical sense, Queen Marie was really "out there" as a person. Her cleavage was big. You see these pictures of her and she is big breasted ... a feminine attribute right in your face. That of course was all highlighted by the clothes that she would wear. But under that outward beauty, the two of them shared this intimacy that love should reign above all things.

According to Bacha, Queen Marie was not one for the rules for royalty. The so-called "lipstick" newsreel of the queen in Chicago is a case in point. In that short film, as the queen is introduced before an audience, she can be seen applying lipstick as she walks on stage. In the clip, she is not at all self-conscious about putting on the lipstick; she certainly made no attempt to hide what she was doing.

Bacha continued:

The fact that they were in Romania and the fact that Romania was under the influence of the Soviet Union was their main reason to go on this trip, which was known as the Peace Tour.
And to try to show that, Queen Marie needed to represent the better part of England to America that Americans were opposed to—the attitude being "we don't want some king telling us what to do." Marie had to show the same kind of compassion, love, and interest in the culture of the people of America she tried to show to Transylvania, and when she had done that to Transylvania, Transylvania got added

to the territory of Romania—this was really the outcome of Queen Marie going to the Paris Peace Conference in 1918.

The Paris Peace Conference and the Treaty of Versailles (1919–1920) enabled the Romanian nation-state to come into being when Transylvania, which had been under Hungarian rule, was united with Romania. Bacha stated:

> This was a declaration but it was also a process … just because they said you are now a part of Romania doesn't mean that the people felt they were Romanian. Queen Marie really tried to incorporate and appreciate all these small courtesies. So she did the same when she came to America. The picture of her in the Native American headdress with the Sioux doesn't tell the complete story. At that time they exchanged a little bit of blood to show that they accepted her as a woman and a blood brother [or sister].

The image of Queen Marie exchanging blood with the Sioux without obsessing on the possible health risks brings to mind a post by Scouting America—or the Boy Scouts of America—that describes the brotherhood blood brother ritual in a piece entitled "Order of the Arrow—Our History":

> Health risk practices are Discontinued for Brotherhood Members:
> In 1956, the National OA Committee, after consultation with medical advisors, determined that it was no longer safe to draw and exchange blood between two people in the "Blood-rite" of the Brotherhood Ceremony.
> The ceremony was changed to only "symbolically" draw blood. Many lodges were very slow in changing this practice of actually pricking the thumb or finger (or in some cases the palm with a knife) and mixing blood between two Arrowmen. There are accounts well into the 1960s of the practice continuing.
> Today all lodges understand that it is a significant health hazard to comingle blood between two people and it is not tolerated at any ritual. The August 1956 Brotherhood Ceremony pamphlet officially incorporated the change from drawing blood to symbolically drawing blood.

During her North American tour, Queen Marie also took part in the Maryhill Museum of Arts dedication ceremony on November 3, 1926. Aside from the general media frenzy that accompanied her everywhere she went, the crowd at the Columbia River Gorge in Goldendale, Washington, where the museum was dedicated, was well over 2,000 strong, including hundreds of schoolchildren and an auto caravan of fans from Portland.

The queen donated more than 100 works of art and personal items to the museum. These gifts can still be seen and include rare paintings, Russian icons, manuscripts, and the gown she wore to the 1896 coronation of her cousins, Tsar Nicholas II and Tsarina Alexandra of Russia.

Bacha commented:

Queen Marie was almost brash with her outwardness. Ileana was a little more afraid: why did she always need angelic protection? Remember, she wrote *The Holy Angels* book. She needed angelic protection because they were at risk of being eliminated.

Queen Marie and Ileana were so close, that was the thing—they were very close ... When she was at the monastery as Mother Alexandra, there was this nun who was literally a thorn in her side— Sister Catherine—living in the same monastery. And so I come along, and Mother Alexandra and I become soul mates, as opposed to the one who doesn't want her to be herself. And yet it was so hard for Sister Catherine because she didn't have any monastic experience. She was guided by Mother Benedicta, the former abbess, who tried to guide Sister Catherine into having a more loving relationship with the Sisterhood, but when it didn't work, Mother Benedicta said, "You gotta leave."

Bacha said that Sister Catherine eventually found a place for herself in Colorado, and that she also went to Romania several times. In Romania she had a little more distance and she got into translations. Sister Catherine was not a people person. Bacha added:

Turns out she had some medical issues that perhaps were indicative of some of the female problems she had. She broke some bones. Perhaps her body lacked calcium. On the whole she didn't have a close association with Mother Alexandra; she resented her royalty. It's odd, but she resented anyone who came to the monastery to talk about Mother Alexandra's royal lineage.

Historian Harry Binkow felt that Mother Alexandra had come to America because her life was being threatened in Paris due to her kinship to royalty and Tsar Nicholas. When I asked Bacha who threatened her life in Paris, she said it was anyone who did not want the royal family to come back:

In Paris she was with Russian nuns. In English they used to call themselves the Protecting Veil of the Virgin Mary, and all of them were there as ex-pats or refugees. The monastics that were there before she arrived were of royal blood ... and being Russian was akin to having a death sentence. Initially Ileana, who became Sister Ileana, never expected to leave Paris and that group. Over time in Paris, the monastery changed. People would come and visit; the monastery was open for hospitality so visitors weren't in an over-guarded environment. When they had written to me and I wrote to them the nuns saw themselves as missionaries. Ileana became the initiator of this new missionary endeavor. Ileana told me that the original plan for her coming to America was that there [were] to be three nuns who would go: Mother Mary (a translator) and Mother Theodora (an older nun), and finally Sister Ileana.

The three nuns became involved in a project to translate the services from Slavonic to English because of Sister Ileana.

Mother Mary had an innate ability to read Greek or Slavonic. She could just write everything out. Sister Ileana didn't understand Slavonic and because of that she didn't know the services. So the translations weren't made for America, they were just made for her. At this time they had no plans to go to America, but then the idea came about that she should go to America.

The nuns figured out that their English translations could attract funding to the new monastery. To do that, they realized they needed some editing of the translations.

That's when Metropolitan Kallistos Ware came in, because Mother Mary's ability was hampered somewhat because she suffered from a mental state: she was bi-polar. Sister Ileana was compassionate enough to be understanding of Mother Mary in her manic state.

The conversation with Bacha then swung back to Queen Marie.

Queen Marie was probably more intimate with Ileana than she was with any other child, even her husband. The spirituality that was in Ileana, that they shared, was somehow in Tsar Nicholas initially when he was faced with the consequences of losing the kingship and the tsardom. This is where the word "transfiguration" comes in. The name "Transfiguration Monastery" points to Ileana wanting to transfigure this into a form of a God-oriented kingdom. The vision that Mother Alexandra didn't want to let go of—in her recounting to me of that 1926 cross-country trip—she never talked about parties or dresses or anything that the news outlets at the time dwelt on. She talked about it more in relation to people.

The plan then was for the three nuns to go to America. Ironically, Bacha said, only Ileana went:

So I became the substitute Mother Mary, the musician, because she didn't have any musical ability at all. We bonded, Mother Alexandra and I, because we both had adversity in our lives.

Mother Alexandra never talked to me about the survival of the Russian Royalty. She talked about the tsar and their summer vacations, where they would get together with his family. And she talked very favorably about it. There was never anything in her conversation that could be considered anti-tsar. The other person that she prayed for a lot was Tsar Alexander I. He was outstanding on her prayer list. You know, this tsar that faked his own death was very important to her.

Historians are uncertain whether Tsar Alexander I faked his own death from typhus in 1825. There are no official documents confirming this fact, although there are many personal testimonies as well as indirect evidence that point to it being true.

The mystery is summarized in a Colorado State University (CSU) collaborative project between CSU and Tomsk Polytechnic University, an outgrowth of the State Department's U.S.–Russia Peer-to-Peer Dialogue Program involving students and faculty. That report states:

The most exciting mystery is connected with the name of Elder Feodor of Tomsk. The history of Saint Feodor of Tomsk begins with the mysterious death of the Russian Emperor Alexander I. Alexander was a fierce critic of his father's policy. His father, the Russian Emperor Paul I was killed on March 11, 1801. Historians still debate Alexander's role in his father's murder. Alexander was deeply affected by his father's death. According to a widespread legend, the Russian emperor Alexander I faked his death in Taganrog in 1825 to become a hermit. The first records of Feodor Kuzmich date back to 1836 when he was arrested for vagrancy in Perm. Feodor Kuzmich had no identity papers on him and after whipping he was exiled to Siberia. He lived in Tomsk for the last 6 years of his life. During the lifetime of Feodor Kuzmich in Siberia there were strong rumors about his being the former emperor. In contrast to how a [*sic*] Emperor would live, Saint Feodor lived a simple life. His home was a small cell with narrow windows. The old man slept on a wooden bed. His clothes were simple. In summer he wore a long white shirt made of village linen. He had only two shirts, belted with a thin strap or rope, and he also wore wide trousers made of linen. In winter he put on a long dark-blue robe over the shirt or if he went out in the cold he put on an old faded Siberian fur coat. His lunch usually consisted of black bread or dried crusts soaked in plain water. Strong arguments that the Elder Feodor was really Alexander I [were] that he knew foreign languages, geography, the history of the War of 1812 (he had defeated Napoleon) and the court life of St. Petersburg.

The CSU report details how the former emperor was allegedly recognized by a former Russian soldier who served with him at the palace in St. Petersburg. It continues:

One former state employee also recognized him and even fainted when she heard a familiar voice. Feodor Kuzmich received a visit from Alexander II in 1837 and his grave was visited by Nicholas II. Moreover, graphology experts have confirmed that the handwriting of Elder Fyodor of Tomsk and that of Tsar Alexander I is identical. Svetlana Semenova, President of the Russian Graphological Society, who analyzed manuscripts written by the emperor and the Elder Fyodor, said that they contain the handwriting of one and the same man.

Throughout his life—whether or not he really was the former tsar—the saintly hermit had a gift of healing and attracted many people with ailments and problems. His relics are kept in the Bogoroditse-Alekseevsky Monastery in Tomsk.

6

Driving Ileana

Everyone assumed she was a Catholic nun.

—Bacha

I asked Bacha if Ileana ever talked about the survival of the Russian nobility. She cited the Tsar Alexander I/hermit story as an example of a tradition of Russian rulers faking their own death in order to invent a new life for themselves.

Tsar Alexander I was the son of Paul I, Emperor of Russia, who ruled from 1796 to 1801, when he was assassinated while in his bedchamber in St. Petersburg. Paul I was the son of Peter III and Catherine the Great, but he was brought up by his father's aunt. Paul never developed a close relationship with his mother. Throughout her life, Catherine kept Paul from participating in government affairs. When Catherine died, Paul reversed many of his mother's laws but in the end he ran afoul of the military, which ultimately led to his demise.

According to Bacha, the story of the survival of Tsar Nicholas and his family "came out in dribbles":

The fact that the tsar and his family survived the execution was so extraordinary it put a real fear in Ileana that she could be done in and maybe even done in within her own household ... She helped Father George Gladky to get here to America. When Father Gladky came to America with his family he would disappear for a week in Virginia or Maryland and go hide for fear of his life in America. This was in the 1980s when the Soviet Union was still intact. It was a fear that didn't go away. For Mother Alexandra it was easier to talk about the angels and stay positive.

Prior to becoming a nun, while she was living in Massachusetts, Ileana needed to support her children so she went on the lecture circuit.

> She loved to travel but she made travel a love because she needed to support her family ... I remember she agreed to come with me to Harrisburg for her first ever women's retreat that I helped schedule. At the retreat she would be talking about women's role in the Orthodox Church. It was a big thing for her to come out like this ... besides the exterior threat [Soviet Union] there was the interior threat of Sister Catherine. Her children actually helped her have a safe place from Sister Catherine ... because she had a retreat house separate from the monastery complex. In 1976, you had to pass the monastery complex to get there ... It wasn't much of a road, maybe 5 feet wide with stones thrown down, enough for a little Volkswagen.

The always cautious but never fearful Ileana was never on the telephone more than ten minutes.

"She didn't fully express herself on the phone and she didn't talk very long," Bacha said. "She was always afraid that someone was tracing the call or listening in. This was not mental paranoia."

Ileana was in the forefront of speakers on the lecture circuit, and women looked up to her because they did not have many Orthodox representatives in those days. "She was more than liberal or conservative; she was unique. For instance, she was definitely for deaconesses in the Orthodox Church," Bacha added.

She said they took a lot of trips by car. Bacha drove Ileana's car, and Ileana decided what trip they would go on. During one road trip to Pittsburgh to do a TV interview, Bacha recalled how they stopped at some shopping mall, got out to walk, and noticed some kiosks with beds for sale.

So all of a sudden she's trying these beds out. Shoppers assumed she was a Catholic nun. She was always being mistaken for a Catholic nun. Later, during the interview, the thing that got journalists' attention was the fact that she was a nun but yet she was a grandmother with grandchildren. Catholic nuns at that time were considered to always be virginal. So she had a lot of explaining to do.

***

We have to get out of our ethnic ghetto to meet the modern World in our own terms.

—Fr. Roman Braga

During the numerous road trips, Bacha said that Ileana treated her as family:

When I drove Ileana I was not yet a nun but a working guest of the monastery. I was also never officially a postulant either. Because of the bad vibes from Sister Catherine, I was pretty much under Mother Alexandra's protection until Mother Benedicta came along and she also took me in. But you know, people were coming to the monastery all the time just to see a real princess. But Sister Catherine didn't want that and she absolutely forbade it. In her latter days, after the fall of the Berlin Wall in 1989, Ileana felt more free to talk about her past and her life as a princess, but prior to that most of her talk was focused on the monastic life. She knew she had to do something about her identity. She was trying to leave discreet historic trails. She was making recordings with me about her life. She had this rich inheritance.

Her last card to me was dated December 1990. She was practically bedridden then. It was written on Saint Nicholas Day. She sent me an icon of the Nativity. At the time I was struggling through issues with my own family relationships regarding my children and she wrote to me about that. "Love will bring them to you in the end," she said. [That prediction proved to be true.] Shortly after this, Ileana fell and broke her hip. Her mobility was more than compromised. But before she broke her hip Ileana was not so much for standing in church; she was sitting—except, of course, for the few times in the service when you had to stand.

She was using a cane at this point and there were many times when she couldn't even attend church services.

In her later years she isolated herself away from the main monastery. This is now the retreat house. In this house there were only two rooms on the main floor. In the main room was a very uncomfortable couch, an historic piece of furniture from her family. When she met people in a public sense she would come out to this room. A double door led into her bedroom [the door that I entered while staying at St. Bridgett's House]. In the bedroom she had a desk and a small portable typewriter. Instead of a wall there was a large sliding glass door so you could see outside. If she was in bed she could pull the curtain and see the outside. She got the bed after her trip to Pittsburgh where all the shoppers in the mall thought she was a Catholic nun. It was a therapeutic bed with hospital features.

The former Abbess of Transfiguration, Mother Elizabeth (not Bacha) died in January 2024, long after her retirement as abbess. She was for many years Ileana's attendant.

Ileana was insistent that the monastery would never experience a day when the nuns were not praying in the morning as well as attending regular liturgies. "This is what monasteries do, you may be thinking—how could it be otherwise?" And yet Ileana had to go out of her way to ascertain this because Sister Catherine did not think the monastery was "prayerful enough."

To solidify the monastery's prayer life, Ileana got Father Roman Braga involved in the cycle of prayers and services. Fr. Braga at the time was pastor of a church in Youngstown, Ohio, very near Ellwood City and near the Pennsylvania border.

Archimandrite Roman Braga felt it was necessary for Orthodoxy to transcend ethnic boundaries in order to enrich its encounter with Western modernity. He wrote:

We have to get out of our ethnic ghetto to meet the modern World in our own terms. We are being challenged today to see the Church no longer primarily in national terms, but as a Eucharistic organism. Our ethnic heritages, however precious, are secondary; the Eucharistic catholicity of the Church comes first. If we continue in isolation, we surely die.

Father Braga was also an advocate for the use of the English language in divine services: "If we use the English language, there would be no problem [in assimilation] because after being in America a year every immigrant should speak at least enough English to understand the liturgy."

In one of his presentations to Orthodox clergy about the process of adaptation to Western modernity, Fr. Roman shared the following thoughts:

Today, not only in the western world, but even in the Orthodox countries, nobody can count on government financial support ... Secularism means that Church and state can no longer be identified. The ethnic boundaries have largely broken down in the west, thank God, and people refer to each other, not as Russian, Romanian or Serbian, but as Orthodox and American. This may seem an impoverishment; but we prefer to regard it as a providential liberation ... Nobody will convert to an "imported religion"; we ourselves act against the growth of Orthodoxy in America, giving the Americans the feeling that Orthodoxy is not the Church of the Fathers but rather something imported from the Orient.

Mother Benedicta, Fr. Braga's sister, was a nun at the Văratec Monastery, one of the largest monasteries in Romania, when she accepted an invitation to be Mother Alexandra's assistant at Transfiguration Monastery. Fr. Braga said:

I stayed there [Transfiguration] 10–12 days and we had discussions regarding monastic life ... I do not believe I was of much help to them. They did not tell me, but they called Bishop Valerian pretending they understood something, that I left them a small ray of light that will shine a little in their hearts. I invited them to visit our monastery to see with their own eyes our way of living with God and for God. To see the beauty of a service, what a monastery with an old tradition looks like ... Will they come? I do not know!

Of that meeting between Mother Benedicta and Ileana, a mutual respect and rapport developed.

The former princess calls for unity

> For Mother Alexandra the door was always open but for Sister
> Catherine the door was always shut!
>
> —Bacha

Ileana had strong pan-Orthodox sensibilities. She wanted unity among
all the Orthodox churches despite chronic geo-political squabbles.
By the same token, she found fault with those Orthodox priests who
refused to pray for non-Orthodox people during Divine Liturgy.

"I can't think of Mother Alexandra not praying for somebody
because they were not Orthodox," Bacha said. She told me a story
about a priest who had a different approach to this question. "Who
do you pray for?" the priest asked. She answered, "Everybody,
because when people die they're all Orthodox."

"Ileana believed in being all together," Bacha said. She was
ecumenical and believed in the unity of the Church.

> Her trip to England was a precursor to her vision of pan-Orthodoxy.
> In England she visited Episcopal churches, Lutheran churches, Russian
> churches. Pan-Orthodoxy wasn't a big thing in 1976 as a movement
> but it was on her agenda so to speak. It was part of what would be
> formative to her coming to America and her vision for the monastery
> to serve English-speaking people in a pan-Orthodox way.

Since Ileana received little help from Orthodox sources in
establishing the monastery, money was forthcoming from the
Women's Anglican Prayer Book Society. Bacha said:

> This was the mainstay outside of her own money and her family's
> money to help the monastery get along when the Orthodox weren't
> sending any money. The Women's Prayer Book Society wasn't fixated
> on them being Anglican or "sacramental."
>
> Prayer was important to Ileana. It was kind of like "Doctors
> Without Borders." It was her global thing, healing and prayer.

Yet Protestant denominations, especially the Episcopal Church,
have changed drastically since 1976. Since that time, standard

Christian biblical beliefs have been altered or subtracted from the canons of that church, so much so that a person from 1970 transported to 2026 to an Episcopal Church during the homily might well be shocked to hear what comes from the pulpit.

While Ileana might have been supportive for deaconesses in the Orthodox Church, one wonders what she might have thought of female priests and bishops who willingly subscribe to what is commonly referred to as a "woke" ideology. A female bishop with blue hair and nose rings decked out in a rainbow stole.

We might ask the same question of Greek Orthodox mystic Vassula Rydén, who died in 2024. Rydén's journey began in November 1985, when she claimed to have received messages from God—her writings are collected in a series of books entitled *True Life in God Messages*—that emphasized unity among Christians until the final goal was achieved: worship around one altar.

Rydén, like Ileana, attended Roman Catholic services, although unlike Ileana, she did not refrain from receiving the sacrament but was insistent that the rules of man are not the rules of God. Equally popular in many Catholic as well as Orthodox communities, Rydén aroused the suspicions and hostility of their respective hierarchies.

In one message about Russia, for instance, Rydén, gives ample proof of the "transcendence of God" when it comes to questions of the "True" Church:

Then, in metaphorical terms, the Lord explained to me that during these years of Communism in Russia and other countries [Romania], they had burnt His Houses (the churches) and became atheists. Then He said that I should stop weeping because He was near Russia right now with His hand on her heart to warm her heart, resurrect her and transfigure her so that she may glorify Him. Not long after that, we heard that Communism in Russia had died: this prophecy came true during the Orthodox Feast of the Transfiguration in August, 1991, with the dissolution of the Soviet Union, which formerly dissolved on December 25, 1991, the commemoration of Christ's birth.

I had received many more prophecies about Russia's return to God, but what struck me most were the prophecies of how she will rise to be the country that will glorify God more than anyone else and that she would be the head of many nations. The Lord strongly expressed Himself of her powerful revival with words such as, "Russia you will live!" These last prophecies, showing that Russia will defend Christianity in a most powerful way, are yet to come.

***

Queen Marie and Ileana's 1926 Peace Tour of North America was scheduled to go through the southern states, but that part of the trip was cancelled not only because of King Ferdinand's health but to fears concerning safety.

"It didn't seem safe enough to go South," Bacha said. "The trip was supposed to bring peace and keep their family safe and alive, but was it safe to say that Nicky [Tsar Nicholas II] and the family were still alive or to delve into any of those issues?"

Was that really going to be safe? Queen Marie had to get home so the trip was cut short. The southern part never happened despite the fact that Queen Marie said she wanted to stretch her hand out of the train window and pick oranges from the orange trees in Florida. There was actually an Orange Hospital in Orlando—the town even changed one of its streets to Ileana Street in honor of the princess. But this trip implanted on Mother Alexandra as a nun a vision of pan-Orthodoxy.

When the Berlin Wall fell in 1989, Bacha continued, people began writing to Ileana from all over the world:

This was also a big part of her ministry—to be in contact with people. She often dictated her letters to me and I would type them. When she first opened Transfiguration some Romanians thought that she should establish the monastery as an old age home. This thought came about when a local priest and his wife were in a car accident, so Ileana as Mother Alexandra did nurse them for a time … this was before I got there. You know, she put her heart into being an abbess but it wasn't easy, especially when you had to direct people in terms of what to do when they didn't want to do it.

7

Survival of the Tsar and his Family

I believe in miracles.
—writer Susan Sontag to a
journalist, 1973

The American essay writer and critic Susan Sontag said:

The problem is that all words were originally religious words. What I mean by "miracle" is that things do happen which are in some ways unmerited or unearned, which defy all odds. This has been used as evidence of the supernatural, but I'm not using it as evidence of anything, except that more is possible than most people imagine and that it makes sense to date to orient your life around the unlikely. The only interesting events, finally, are miracles—those moments when things leap out of themselves. That's what most of great literature is about. But most books that feel modern have been about a miracle not happening. *Madame Bovary*, for instance. It's about somebody wanting something different but being absolutely incapable of producing it because of the corruption and insignificance, finally, of the heroine's circumstances and imagination. All that's told with the greatest sympathy, but, nevertheless, Madame Bovary's imagination is corrupt. Her folly is inspired by vulgar models which can never support her fantasies and make them come true. So, she's a dupe, and she doesn't understand what she's doing.

Sontag, who died in 2004, went on to say:

A lot of art in the last hundred years has been about people not managing to do what they want because they haven't made the proper kind of spiritual effort.

That's what attracts me in works of art and in life—the absence or presence of a miracle. I don't think of it as something religious. Though you could explain it in religious terms, any terms which go beyond a demeaning and reductive analysis of human existence have to take account of the unpredictable and wholly extraordinary. But I don't mean to suggest that all miracles are good.

Ileana's reinvention of herself as a monastic after two marriages, the raising of a family, and an earlier life as a Romanian royal among the courts of Europe—where she was a favorite playmate of the tsar's son, Alexei, so much so that many at the time assumed the two would eventually marry—suggests a miracle of personal transfiguration.

Bacha stated:

Queen Marie needed to have peace and be a proponent for peace (and her personal survival) in the situation she and her country were in. The transcendentalists and the Bahai faith and maybe more try to claim her while she was trying to maintain a delicate diplomacy. Yes, Marie was interested in the Bahai faith, as she was also in Islam and other things. It all amounted to an education, but these things did *not* become her personal religious creed according to Mother Alexandra. Queen Marie, we must not forget, converted to Russian Orthodoxy in 1926.

Bacha points to Tolstoy and how he was also manipulated in this time.

We do not hear on Martin Luther King Day that Gandhi was so very interested in Tolstoy. Tolstoy? Yes, Tolstoy wrote him letters, one labeled "to a HINDU." Tolstoy told Gandhi the best thing he could do in India for peace was to become an Orthodox Christian!

Marie of Romania was very interested in Tolstoy. But she also needed to be published as a pacifist and as an advocate for peace.

When she had no voice for publication and she needed to publish, she went to the Bahais for this work or this call to peace.

Writer Martha Root describes her meeting with Queen Marie in the April 1936 edition of *The Bahá'í World*:

The first Queen of the world to study and to promote Bahá'u'lláh's great Teachings has been Her Majesty Queen Marie of Rumania, one of the queens of this twentieth century who stands highest in intellect, in vision, in clear understanding of the new universal epoch now opening. Her Majesty received the book *Bahá'u'lláh and the New Era* by Dr. J. E. Esslemont and a note from the writer of this article who first visited Bucharest, Rumania, in January, 1926. The Rumanian Queen, granddaughter of the renowned Queen Victoria of the British Empire and of Czar Alexander II of Russia, both of whom received Tablets from Bahá'u'lláh in their day, read this volume until three o'clock in the morning and two days later, on January 30, 1926, received me in audience in Cotroceni Palace, in Bucharest. Her first words after the greeting were, "I believe these Teachings are the solution for the world's problems today!" The account of that historic morning appeared in *The Bahá'í Magazine* in Washington, in June, 1926, but very illuminating letters written by Her Majesty that same year show how deep was her confirmation. Here is one written to her beloved friend Loie Fuller, an American then residing in Paris, which after these ten years can be published for the first time:

"Lately great hope has come to me from one, Abdu'l-Bahá, a personal follower of Christ. Reading, I have found in His and His Father Bahá'u'lláh's Message of Faith all my yearnings for real religion satisfied. If you ever hear of Bahá'ís or of the Bahá'í Movement which is known in America you will know what that is! What I mean, these books have strengthened me beyond belief and I am now ready to die any day full of hope; but I pray God not to take me away yet, for I still have a lot of work to do."

Root also describes meeting Princess Ileana:

Meeting the Queen again on January 19, 1928, in the Royal Palace in Belgrade, where she and H.R.H. Princess Ileana were guests of the Queen of Jugoslavia—and they had brought some of their Bahá'í books with them—the words I shall remember longest of all that Her dear Majesty said were these: "The ultimate dream which we shall realize is that the Bahá'í channel of thought has such strength, it will serve little by little to become a light to all those searching for the real expression of Truth."

8

A Rendezvous?
Tsar Nicholas II and Queen Marie

When I go out on the street now, I look all around just to make sure
I'm not being followed by some mug. Yes. They want me dead. Well
so what! The fools don't understand who I am. A sorcerer? Well,
perhaps. They burn sorcerers, so let 'em go ahead and burn me. One
thing they don't understand: if they kill me, it's the end of Russia.
They'll bury us together.

—Grigori Rasputin

So, Princess Ileana, Mother Alexandra is the blood daughter of Tsar
Nicholas 11 and Queen Marie of Romania.

—Bacha

It happened at the wedding of Grand Duchess Maria Pavlovna, 18, and
Prince Wilhem of Sweden, 23, in St. Petersburg in September 1908.

Maria Pavlovna was the only daughter and the eldest of two
children of Grand Duke Paul Alexandrovich of Russia and Princess
Alexandra of Greece and Denmark. Prince Wilhem, known as the
"sailor prince" due to his service in the Swedish Navy, met Maria
when she was 16 years old. He knew the day after meeting her
that he wanted to marry her. Maria was quite plump when she met
the tall, thin prince with long artistic fingers and piercing brown
eyes. Their engagement was aided by the Grand Duchess of Sege,
Elizabeth—or "Aunt Ella"—(who became a nun and who is now
a saint in the Russian Orthodox Church), Maria's godmother and
the woman who raised her.

Maria's godmother was named after Elizabeth of Hungary (1207–1231), a Catholic saint in her own family, although she was born into a Lutheran family. Elizabeth's mother died when she was a girl; she was then sent to England to live with her grandmother, Queen Victoria, who brought her up as an Anglican. After her marriage to Grand Duke Sergei Alexandrovich, one of Tsar Alexander II's five sons, she converted to Russian Orthodoxy.

Life changed for Elizabeth on February 18, 1905, when her husband was assassinated. She became a very devout woman, giving away all her possessions and putting her faith into action when she opened up the Martha and Mary home in Moscow. By 1909 she and seventeen other women had become nuns, the Sisters of Love and Mercy.

After the Bolshevik revolution in May 1918, Elizabeth was arrested along with two nuns from her convent and taken to Alapaevsk. A day after the tsar and his family were allegedly shot dead on July 17, Elizabeth and another nun from Saints Mary and Martha, as well as distant members of the royal family, were murdered in a mineshaft.

Not only did Aunt Ella foster a relationship and campaign for a marriage between Maria Pavlovna and Prince Wilhelm, she engineered a special meeting between Tsar Nicholas II and Queen Marie during the wedding of Maria.

According to Bacha, who stated that she got the story directly from Ileana—who got it from her mother, Queen Marie—this is what occurred.

While it is true that the Empress Alexandra was in St. Petersburg for the pre-marriage robing ceremony, she did not attend the wedding ceremony itself, leaving Nicholas without his Alexandra.

That wedding was quite a spectacular event.

Maria Pavlovna created quite a stir in her wedding dress of silver brocade cut to her shoulders, with gemstones sewn into the dress's dramatic sleeves. The material-heavy ensemble included a long train of ermine-trimmed velvet, standard fare for Romanov brides since the 1830s and extremely heavy to carry. The weight was so oppressive it took five chambermaids to help carry the train.

Maria wore a 13 carat Paul I pink diamond tiara, a crown originally made for Tsar Alexander I's wife, Elizabeth Alexeievna.

Mounted behind the tiara was the Romanov Nuptial Crown. But by far the heaviest items of jewelry on Maria were the diamond cherry earrings, so weighty they took two thick wires so they could sashay safely as the bride walked. These cumbersome face chandeliers proved extremely irksome over the long haul, so Maria removed them at the reception and placed them both over the rim of her water glass.

Accounts from *The Court Jeweler*, a popular online blog devoted to stories of royalty, tell us how the diamond necklace Maria wore contained stones cut during the reign of Catherine the Great. The bride also wore a four-studded diamond bracelet.

While the official guest list included Nicholas II, Alexandra and her daughters, the groom's parents, and Ferdinand and Marie of Romania, Alexandra did not attend the ceremony. Her absence provided the perfect segue for a secret rendezvous between Nicholas and Queen Marie. This meeting was set up by Aunt Ella to ensure a healthy male heir to the Russian throne, as Alexei was already suffering from hemophilia and was not expected to live very long. A healthy male heir had to be found, and a match between Nicholas II and Queen Marie seemed to provide the perfect solution.

Queen Marie was considered the most beautiful royal in Europe. She is described as having a ready wit and "sparkling blue eyes and silky fair hair." Before her marriage to Ferdinand, she was courted by many royal bachelors, including Prince George of Wales. Nicholas, of course, had his own dashing qualities. Many referred to him as the "handsomest man in all Europe" with his reddish-brown hair, Grecian nose, and imperial bearing. At 5ft 6in., he was not as tall as most males in the Romanov family; his body type was more like the petite frame of his mother, Maria Feodorovna.

The commingling—or the coming together—of Queen Marie and Nicholas at the Pavlovna wedding must have played out sometime before or after the ceremony. Perhaps it occurred during the reception celebrations; one can imagine Queen Marie scurrying to meet Nicholas in some secret room or chamber, with Aunt Ella— her sainthood not yet fully ripe—guarding the door or hallways as the two royals eased into a business embrace *sans* real romance (if we are to believe Bacha) in order to produce a healthy male heir.

This conjugal coming together was for the good of the nation, the hope being that a male child would spring forth who would grow up and be healthy without needing a Rasputin to perform healing miracles every time he got sick.

The intimate details of this alleged union will forever be a mystery, yet one thing is certain: if it occurred at all, once the merger was consummated the two royals went their separate ways. Aunt Ella took the details of the secret rendezvous to her grave. Questions remain, however. What about the arrangements surrounding switching the baby at birth if Marie's pregnancy resulted in the birth of a boy? And what of King Ferdinand, her husband—how would he not notice his wife's pregnancy, unless of course Queen Marie and he had a consistent healthy marital relationship so that a pregnancy would not be a total surprise? The assumption would be that the child Marie was carrying was his.

In any event, a male child to "replace" Alexei was not produced. Instead, Ileana was born, the daughter—at least according to Bacha—of Tsar Nicholas II and Queen Marie. Bacha told me:

Mother Alexandra as Princess Ileana was a planned conception at the time of the wedding of Maria Pavlovna. Maria, the godchild of my namesake St. Elizabeth, the Grand Duchess Sege [Sergei]—or as Mother Alexandra would call her, "Aunt Ella"—arranged for this union when Tsarina Alexandra did not attend the wedding ... So Princess Ileana, Mother Alexandra, is the blood daughter of Tsar Nicholas II and Queen Marie of Romania.

Breaking news, indeed...

As for plump Maria Pavlovna's marriage to the thin, dark-haired prince with the long artistic fingers, that did not turn out so well.

As a naval officer, the prince was away from home more than he was by Maria's side. It did not help that Maria found it hard to adjust to Swedish court life, a much more formal environment than the Russian court. After the birth of the couple's son, Lennart, in 1909, Maria left her husband and returned to Russia. This created a major scandal. Before establishing herself in Paris, Maria eked out a living for herself in Russia by writing icons and coloring wooden Easter eggs. Eventually, Maria opened an embroidery shop in Paris that became quite popular, attracting the likes of Coco Chanel, who became a regular patron. Maria rarely saw her son, Lennart instead living with his father. Essentially, she abandoned both husband and family.

In Paris, she was joined by her brother, Grand Duke Dmitri Pavlovich, who was one of Rasputin's assassins and who wound up having a love affair with Coco Chanel. Pavlovich, a first cousin of Nicholas II, later regretted his involvement in the death of the faith healer and mystic. Yet as Douglas Smith explains in his book *Rasputin: Faith, Power, and the Twilight of the Romanovs*, "Rasputin's killers all shared the belief that they were preparing for an act of noble patriotism, but other motives were in play as well." Pavlovich's participation, Smith writes, "must also be explained in part by his desire to please Ella," the future saint. "She was like a second mother to him, and it was only after a lengthy conversation with her that Dimitri agreed that murder was the right course of action."

The saintly nun prays for Rasputin's murder

After Rasputin was killed, Douglas Smith writes that Ella returned to Moscow on the evening of the 17th from Sarov, where she had gone to spend a week in prayer for Dimitri and fellow murderer Prince Felix Yusupov, whom she called her "darlings." [Rasputin's other murderers were Lieutenant Sergei Sukhotin, Vladimir Purishkevich, and Doctor Stanislaus Lazovert.]

After praying for a successful murder, Smith writes that the next morning Ella, the future saint, sent two telegrams, the first to Felix's mother, "blessing the actions of her son and sending him and the entire family her prayers." She then sent a telegram to Dimitri, "asking that he send her a letter with all the details of the 'patriotic deed.'" Smith continues:

> Both telegrams were intercepted by the police ... and delivered to the imperial palace. Later that month Ella told Dimitri's sister on her way through Moscow how thrilled she was with Rasputin's murder and that Providence had deigned to select her brother and Felix ... Neither the Holy Synod nor the Russian Orthodox Church

condemned Rasputin's murder or the [eventual] desecration of his grave.

Smith quotes from Dimitri's diary his confession that he had only participated in the murder "to give poor Niki [Nicholas] one last chance—so that he could change political course ... From this it clearly follows that I took part in this affair out of my desire to help the Emperor, out of my loyalty to him, and not for the sake of my own popularity." Dimitri concludes: "But many were of the opinion that I was a candidate for the throne, they said that the Rasputin affair was a trampoline or spring board that would put me on the throne."

As punishment for his participation, Dimitri was exiled from the Russian Court and transferred to an obscure military post in Persia. Dimitri's family objected to the punishment and wrote a collective letter to Nicholas II imploring him to rescind the sentence, claiming that isolating him in Persia was tantamount to a death sentence. But Nicholas could not be moved, sending the letter back to the family with these words: "No one has been given the right to practice murder, and I know that many are troubled by their conscience, for Dimitri Pavlovich is not the only one involved in this. I'm surprised by your appeal to me."

One wonders if Nicholas II had Sister Elizabeth (Aunt Ella) in mind when he wrote: "I know that many are troubled by their conscience."

The Empress Alexandra, as well as Alexei, wanted Nicholas II to hang the murderers. They did not see Rasputin as an enemy of the state and did not believe the sensationalist tales about the mystic-healer.

"It was rumored at the time when Nicholas refused to execute Rasputin's killers as Alexandra had demanded, she slapped him across the face," Smith writes.

It was also true that Nicholas almost always welcomed Rasputin's visits to the palace. According to Smith, Nicholas recorded in his diary on October 17, 1915, of having been in a "beastly mood" all day "due to the actions of the Germans and the Turks on the Black Sea ... But that evening Rasputin came and all was better: 'Only under the influence of Grigory's calming talk did my soul return to its normal balance!'"

For his part, Dimitri was filled with such hatred over the order to send him to Persia that he wrote in his diary: "Alexandra Fyodorovna is victorious, but will that scum hold power for long?! And what sort of man is he, he disgusts me, yet still I love him, for he does not have a bad soul."

Another of Rasputin's murderers—and a "darling of" Aunt Ella's—Prince Felix Yusupov, made no secret of his fantasies, according to Smith, "of murdering Nicholas's wife."

Ironically, Dimitri's exile to Persia ended in his escape to London, and in 1926 he married Anna Audrey Emery, an American heiress. He died on March 5, 1942, aged 50 in Davos, Switzerland. His son, Prince Pavel (Paul) Romanov-Ilyinsky (1928–2004), became the mayor of Palm Beach, Florida.

In many biographies of the Russian royal family, a kind of sanitized hagiography comes into play when the life of Aunt Ella (Sister Elizabeth) is discussed.

A May 2025 blog, *The Inner Things*, by traditionalist Catholic-turned Russian Orthodox writer Michael Warren Davis, features the life of Sister Elizabeth but completely overlooks the nun's passive and quite unsaintly "participation" in the murder of Rasputin. Davis writes:

> In 1981, Elizabeth and Alexandra were raised to the altars by the Holy Synod of the Russian Church. Why did Elizabeth do what she did? She had no terrible sin to repent of, no secret shame. She remained faithful to her husband even after discovering that he had taken dozens of young men as lovers throughout their married life. She was generous to the poor even before her husband's death. She was even a vegetarian.
>
> Maybe there's a political message here. Had the Russian aristocracy been more like Elizabeth, the Bolsheviks never would have seized power. When Sergei became Governor General of Moscow, his first act was to expel the Jews from the city. She begged him to show mercy—just as she begged Tsar Nicholas to forgive Sergei's murderer.

As for Maria Pavlovna, from Paris she embarked on a globetrotting spree, living in the United States and Argentina. She married a second time to Sergei Mikhailovich, but that ended in divorce in

1923. She died on December 13, 1958, in West Germany, near her son Lennart and his family.

According to Carol Bacha:

Grand Duchess Maria Pavlovna could have been a good princess of Sweden but she refused to cooperate. As an early nineteenth-century royal she expected too much from a dynastic marriage. She could have found comfort in her son and encouraged him to make a dynastic marriage. If that had been the case, his descendent would probably now be in line of succession to the Swedish crown, but she rather chose the shameful divorce and to exile herself from her homeland, then exile herself again from Russia and keep moving from one continent to another.

Prince Wilhelm's life in many ways did not really begin until after Maria deserted him. Yet early indications of trouble in the union can be seen in their official wedding portrait. The picture clearly indicates a psychic estrangement between them. Wilhelm, his hands folded over his groin, looks as though he is about to take a dose of unpleasant medicine, while Maria seems decidedly distant and skeptical.

After the divorce, Wilhelm met a French woman, Jeanne de Tramcourt, who was then estranged from her Swedish sculptor husband, who liked using her as a model. In most pictures, Jeanne de Tramcourt bears an uncanny resemblance to Maria Pavlovna, indicating what may have attracted Wilhelm to her in the first place. Their life together was stable, Jeanne living with Wilhelm in his new home, Stenhammar Palace, in Flen, Sweden. The two did not marry, given the restrictions stemming from Wilhelm's royal status—Tramcourt was a commoner—but that did not prevent them from living together. Tramcourt, while not recognized as Wilhelm's wife, would instead come to be known as the "hostess of Stenhammar."

The couple's life together, however, would end when Tramcourt was killed in an automobile accident in 1952. They were on their way to visit Wilhelm's son, Lennart, when snowy conditions on the road caused the car to slide and crash. Wilhelm, the driver, blamed himself for the crash for the rest of his life.

After the death of Jeanne, Wilhelm surrounded himself with writers and artists at Stenhammar. He died of a heart attack on June 5, 1965, just twelve days before his 81st birthday. A poet and filmmaker, the tall, thin man with the long artistic fingers wrote more than forty books, many of them travel volumes about Central America, Thailand. and Africa. He is buried in the Polish cemetery in Flen, Sweden.

***

Grigori Rasputin left a letter to his family that was found after his murder by his daughter, Maria. It read as follows:

My dears,

A disaster is threatening us, a great misfortune is drawing near. The face of Our Lady has darkened and the spirit is disturbed in the calm of night. This calm will not last. Terrible will be the wrath. And whither shall we flee? It is written: Watch, for you know neither the day nor the hour. This day has come for our country. There will be cries and blood. In the great darkness of these griefs I can now distinguish nothing. My hour will soon strike. I am not afraid, but I know it will be bitter. I shall suffer and it will be pardoned to men. I shall inherit the kingdom, but you will be saved. The road of your sufferings is known to God. Men without number will perish. Many martyrs will die. Brothers will be slain by their brothers. The earth will tremble. Famine and pestilence will reign, signs will appear to men. Pray for your salvation. And through the grace of the Saviour and of Her who intercedes with Him you will be consoled.

Grigori

Smith contends that this prediction of coming disaster is not truly prophetic, because by December 1916, "many Russians could see the bloody revolution staring them in the face." Smith goes on to say that Rasputin's "knowledge of his approaching death is striking and cannot be argued away" and that maybe Rasputin "did indeed foresee the violent end just around the corner." This can be seen as an admission that the mystic-healer was indeed a prophet.

As Archpriest Andrew Phillips writes in *Orthodox Christianity* ("The Real Gregory Rasputin"):

He was certainly not mad, never a priest, monk, thief or spy, never a flagellant sectarian or a Satanist, and had very little if any political influence. He was a pious Christian peasant, married with three children, who gave generous alms, understood the Holy Scriptures better than professors of the Bible, and was so pious that God gave him miraculous powers of healing ... He was murdered by British spies, with the co-operation of rich, decadent, jealous and apostate Russian aristocrats, one transvestite prince who dabbled in the occult and savagely and ritually battered Gregory Rasputin's corpse, as the sadistic freemason and decadent Prince Yusupov himself boasted of doing, one a more or less Fascist politician, another a Romanov prince of notoriously loose morals who betrayed his relative the Tsar.

In the book, *The Mad Monk of Russia: Life, Memoirs, and Confessions of Sergei Michailovich Trufanoff (Iliodor)*, published in 1918, we get two views of Rasputin. Iliodor as a young man was at first convinced of the saintliness of Rasputin and became his fiercest advocate. He also became a priest and a monk but later on turned against Rasputin and after the latter's death left the priesthood, married and migrated to America where he became a kind of ad hoc Marxist revolutionary, advocating for the elimination of the aristocratic classes. Iliodor, upon his arrival in New York City, was interviewed by a government official from Russia who asked him about his work history. Iliodor described himself as an "unskilled laborer," adding, "You must not forget that for twenty years I held in my hands nothing but a pen and a cross. I found that I was getting more than I could give, and I left."

He then goes on to say, "I left the factory because I did not know how to work. Workmen who know their business should stay in the factory and see that their superiors do not take too much advantage of them. If labor were paid justly and humanly, there would be no palaces and there would be no slums."

In one 1917 New York photograph, the former monk, dressed in a bow tie—and a little overweight I might add—looks like a disgruntled leftwing activist. The former monk also admits in the Epilogue to the book, that Rasputin, "In his nature possessed much which is as yet unknown, and with these unknown potentialities he was able to obtain ascendancy over many people. One of them was the power to receive prophetic dreams in which he foresaw the future, and these prophetic dreams of his were not of secondary importance among his occult powers. As for myself, I also have these dreams, but rarely…" Here Iliodor seems to let the cat out of the bag, for he is still mostly uncertain about his mentor's spiritual powers, despite the slings and arrows he levels at Rasputin throughout the book.

Iliodor proceeds to write what Rasputin once told him about his visits to the palace:

"Don't imagine that it is easy to talk to rulers. No, it is hard. The blood clots one's lips; one shrinks from giving them counsel. But they consult me about everything. It may be hard on them to have to listen to a peasant, but listen they do. Once the czar said, 'Be it so,' and I replied, 'No, not so.' His cheeks became flushed, he began to tremble; you see, he did not like the idea of obeying a peasant, but he obeyed just the same. He cannot even breathe without me….When I visited them after the suppression of the revolution, both the czar and the czarina knelt before me and began to kiss my hands and feet. The czarina raised her hands heavenward and said, with eyes full of tears, 'Gregory, even though all the men on earth rise against you, I shall not leave you, and I shall listen to nobody.' And the czar, also raising his hands, exclaimed, 'Gregory, you are Christ!'"

9

Interview with (Prince) Dominic Habsburg

Romanians are not known for their honesty. I have no prejudices
myself, except gypsies. Stealing is a part of their trade, culture.

—Prince Dominic Habsburg

I am journeying to meet a real prince, Dominic von Habsburg,
member of the Grand Ducal Family of Tuscany and the House of
Habsburg-Lorraine, whose grandparents were Queen Marie and
King Ferdinand of Romania and his parents Princess Ileana of
Romania and Archduke Anton of Austria.

Dominic, or "Niki" as he is referred to in books about Queen
Marie, was born on July 4, 1937, in Hollabrunn, Austria. He is
the sole surviving son of Princess Ileana, who later became Mother
Alexandra, the Orthodox nun who founded the Monastery of the
Transfiguration in Ellwood City, Pennsylvania. The Habsburgs—who
rose to prominence in the Holy Roman Empire and had their family
seat at Habsburg Castle, built in the eleventh century—became one
of the most influential dynasties in European history. With their vast
territorial holdings, they wielded immense political power.

I was given Dominic's contact information from Mother
Christophora, abbess of Transfiguration, who told me she had
never met him and was not sure whether he had ever even visited
the monastery. I watched as Mother Christophora dug through
an old rolodex and copied out his address for me. Later, I wrote
Dominic a note requesting an interview; he called me soon after.
We settled on a date when I would take Amtrak to New York City

from Philadelphia, transfer to Grand Central Station, and then take the commuter rail Metro North Railroad Harlem Line to Purdys, New York, where Dominic would be waiting for me.

It was a bright, sunny fall early afternoon when the train pulled into Purdys station. I had seen pictures of Dominic on the web, so I knew basically who I was looking for: a tall, lean gentleman with a crown of white hair. Dominic's face lit up with a relaxed smile when we spotted one another. It was a smile that in some ways spelled relief. I was a little concerned that we might not get along, that there would be a chemistry misalignment, and that the interview would go terribly wrong.

Extending his hand, Dominic said almost immediately: "You look like an old school chum of mine in Austria!" We laughed. Once in his car, the conversation became casual. He had just been to see the dermatologist—another appointment, he lamented—stemming from all the years he spent in the Caribbean. Sun damage; how well I knew that mantra. We drove through beautiful countryside, making small talk, his strong accent never clouding his words.

Architect, designer, an alumnus of the Brooks School and the Rhode Island School of Design, he is no peacock prince, but a prince who works and has a number of patents for inventions—some ten inventions, he says. He would even tell me later how he was hoodwinked out of patent royalties because his business helper at the time had the contract drawn up in French: "So I never got royalties although in my life I've made plenty of money."

In the car, he tells me about a Danish-style piece of furniture he designed, "a couch that turns into a bed with the mechanism made into the parts—not separate—but nobody was interested in the prototype, so it never got made." He said he later became a sort of clearinghouse for patents; he had this innate ability to know whether inventions would work.

Dominic pulls into his gated driveway, pushes a button, and the gates open wide. He designed the house himself. It is all on one level, reminiscent of Frank Lloyd Wright and Philip Johnson. It is built around a large garden-atrium in the center. The constant light source electrifies the interior design, especially in the living and dining areas, where masterful European portraits of kings, queens, and other royal personages in serious museum-style frames greet the visitor.

"These are all family members," he tells me, pointing to the portraits.

I notice a very large wooden statue on a bookshelf. It is the statue of St. Benedict in which his mother—the princess and later the nun—writes about in her memoir, *I Live Again*. Dominic informs me that as a child he used to run his hands up and down the sculpted folds of the saint's robes when the statue was in Bran Castle. Instinctively, I run my hands along the wooden folds. This is no ordinary statue, because Benedict seems to be burying his head into his chest. He is either praying or mourning the loss of something.

We head back to the car again, off to lunch at the Farmer and the Fish restaurant, located in an eighteenth-century house. I spent time photographing some of the magnificent portraits on the walls. Dominic confesses he gets uneasy when people photograph the interior of his house, namely the portraits, because one can never be sure where the pictures will wind up. Such publicity may invite thieves. We live in strange times. At the restaurant, several heads turn as we enter; a couple of people say "hello" to Dominic. We opt for an outside table, because inside it is noisy.

At the table, I ask Dominic whether he can verify a claim made in one biography of his mother—*Royal Monastic: Princess Ileana of Romania (The Story of Mother Alexandra)* by Bev Cooke—that during the toughest times, as the communists were gaining control of the country, Ileana had a stash of secret suicide pills to distribute to herself and her children so that the family would not suffer unnecessarily.

If it's true, I don't know where it came from. This is the first time I'm hearing this. My mother and suicide: it doesn't add up. It doesn't fit her at all. If she had occasional thoughts, I don't know. I've had suicidal thoughts when I was young. Then I thought, well, I'm going to die anyway so why not wait and see how it all turns out. I've told that to people and it saved their lives. You're going to die anyway, so why take your life?

My mother was an extremely proud woman, very selfish in her own way. She treated her children as if they were extensions of herself. She was very self-assured in her own way. She grew up as an important person among kings and queens. She had an extreme sense of duty. Her religious beliefs were very much like my grandmother's [Queen Marie].

We discuss Ileana's relationship with her mother, Queen Marie.

Her mother played a great role in her development. They were very close. She was the favorite child. Why did my mother have six children? Because her mother had six children. She admired her mother to that degree. The Queen had a sense of "I am." So did the princess. I am the Princess. I am the Archduchess. I am the Mother Superior."

I ask Dominic what it was like when his mother announced she wanted to become a nun.

When she became a nun it didn't fit into the concept of my mother at all. She was much too independent to go into such a confined atmosphere. She was … [Dominic hesitates as if trying to find the words.] She was drawn to monastic life; in the end it was her salvation. She was centered in religion as was her mother but my mother probably took it more seriously. We had in the house growing up [in Newton] a friend of hers who was a Christian Scientist, and she had her there because she was interested in it. She was drawn into religion.

When my mother decided to become a nun—you have to remember that we came out of the war, she had six children and she sent them to the best schools to see that they got a very good education. Having to do something was always very important. I asked how she was going to survive. I said, "I can't see you on a street corner and asking for donations." Of course she would get very mad at me. She would say working for God and Christ is good and what is given is charity. I asked her, "What is this monastery going to do?" She said, "We're going to translate the liturgy and things like that." I said, "For that you don't need a convent, you need a good translator, you don't need to become a nun. Why do you want to go into this monastery?" I was very hard on her. She threw it right back at me.

Dominic talked about being the "leader" of the second set of three children, while his brother Stefan led the older first set of three. "My brother Stefan felt he was the big brother of everybody, while I being the leader of the lower ones didn't feel I was the leader of anybody." He described himself as a boy observer. He then delved into his parents' divorce.

> When my parents divorced, I asked the question why? They had six children. They went through all of this hell. Why divorce? Actually, I don't know why my father didn't divorce my mother because she treated him terribly.

This hit me like a small bombshell. Dominic goes on to mention Hannah Pakula's 1984 book *The Last Romantic: A Biography of Queen Marie of Romania*:

> In the book *The Last Romantic*, I hear my mother speaking ... but my mother was the major source for this book. She contacted me first after the author contacted her, but when I read her book, in the author's descriptions of my father I hear my mother talking ... Both Queen Marie and my mother considered men inferior. Well, my grandfather, King Ferdinand, was a good man but he was boring ... very straight and narrow-minded. She was bored by her husband. Queen Marie and King Ferdinand had affairs. Queen Marie married at 17 and she didn't know what lovemaking was all about. She even says this in her own book. When she went to bed with King Ferdinand, she didn't know what the hell she was doing.

Our conversation shifts back to religion. In her autobiography (1934), Queen Marie wrote:

> Ileana was certainly the child of my soul. Her large dark blue eyes looked at you with deep inquiry and the child seemed to understand your every emotion with almost uncanny lucidity. It was never necessary to teach Ileana the difference between right and wrong; she knew.

Ileana, Dominic says, was deeply affected when her youngest brother, Mircea, died at the age of 3 of typhoid fever. (The Romanian Royal family are buried in the Curtea de Argeş Cathedral in the Curtea de Argeş Monastery.) "My mother says she saw angels standing by his bed. Those things I won't go into because I can tell you experiences of my own. I have no proof: was I hallucinating?"

I don't press Dominic to elaborate on his experiences in that realm, but listen closely as he explains that he does not like to get involved in religious discussions in general.

Ninety percent of religion you cannot prove. The things that we argue about are ridiculous. Like the Virgin Mary ... whether she was a virgin or not is absolutely irrelevant ... for some people being a virgin makes it holy and for other people it makes the story human.

I had some good times with my father [Archduke Anton of Austria].

But there were big differences in character between them. My father mistrusted everybody but when he trusted somebody it was real. So there's a danger there, too. My mother loved everybody and was deeply hurt. She took two Romanians with her when she left the country in 1948, one fellow and another fellow who was an investor ... so the last money that my mother still had outside in trusts, she let him administrate it and it all went straight into his pocket. My father at the time was desperate. And he told me this afterwards, many years later, that "this man, this administrator, is ruining you. When will you come to your senses? So, if she loses all her money it's worth it, just so she will come to her senses." Of course she never did. But he embezzled everything. This is part of my own research. It's not in *The Last Romantic*, as to why they separated. Why did they divorce after being together for so long? She instigated the divorce proceedings. I have this letter at home regarding this.

See, I feel that she becoming a nun in the end was "I am." What else could she have done? She lost everything. She lost the kingdom. She lost her marriage. Where was she supposed to go? I used to say to King Michael all the time when he was in England—he was much older than me—"You can't put an ad in the paper or make a telephone call: King looking for a job." King Michael went through hell. Living in poverty; who would give him a job? And I lived it, when I first came to the United States. When I got back into Austria in 1960, the country—it was just after the war; Europe was picking itself up but it was a wonderful time—the spirit was forward-looking, there was enthusiasm, but for me to get a job was very difficult. So the name—people said well, with your name you can go anywhere, but it doesn't get you the job. They didn't give me the work. From the political side, I found out very quickly that I could work much better with socialists than with the conservatives. One side wanted to show us they were for us, the other side wanted to show us they were against us.

And then I had Anglo-Saxon training. I wanted to get in somewhere but I couldn't get in through the front door ... I'll go through the window and if you can't go through the window, I'll go down the chimney. But I'll get in ... somehow. That was my attitude. I went back to Austria, a country I had no relationship with whatsoever. My father gave me my first job, surveying, as his technical assistant in foresting. But he allowed me to go and do something on my own. And since everything was building up there was a demand for design. A different sort of thinking was in the air. But there are a number of designers in Austria, two in particular, that always give me credit for their creations. I opened the door for a lot of designers. I didn't get upset if I didn't get the job, I just got another one ... And I worked all through Europe.

Dominic surprises me when he says: "Ask me something more about the mother."

The choice of words was curious; "the mother" is intoned as if it represented a tall White or Nordic visitor out of a Whitley Strieber narrative.

Nonetheless, I asked: "Did your mother ever spank you?"

My mother basically lived her own life. I never got a spanking. She did what she had to do, public service, and in Romania she had a hospital [Hospital of the Queen's Heart] where she worked all day. And we had a nanny who would slam me down on toilets and whip me with a stick—yes, that's what the nanny did—and she had an assistant who would take my older sister and beat her every night. So the children grew up with nannies or "other people."

"Did you ever tell your mother about the nanny?"

I don't think I ever told my mother about the nanny who beat me. The worst story in that sense was when we were in Austria and I was 4 or 5, and this man put my brother over a chair and beat him with a riding crop, and then he would ask my sisters "how many more times should I hit him?" Then he came at me. He asked me for a number. For some reason I said nine. It was the first number that appeared in my head. So my brother was beaten nine times because of my stupidity. My sisters were all saying to me, "How could you? How could you?" But my brother who was beaten stood up for me. The person closest to my mother was my brother. She shared everything with him. To the end, until she died. He was there for her, and they were there for each other.

Dominic is not one to mince words when he talks about his family.
    "I talked to my brother ages ago about his wife, and said if I had a wife like that I would have divorced her. He said, 'No, I took on the responsibility.'"
Dominic mentions that his sister-in-law is upset with him.

She [my sister-in-law] adored my mother in everything and she copied her … she even wore those salesgirl-style glasses with straps on the ears, as did my mother. She visited me in Austria and I had just moved there. And my little sister came a bit later. Somehow we got on the subject that somebody has to look after this younger sister. Then we got on the subject of my mother's relationship with the children. Her favorite and most important in the family was my brother Stefan. His wife said, "Oh that's not true."
    My sister Minola was my father's favorite. And the rest of us just came somewhere along the line. And I described each one of the children to my sister-in-law. My middle sister has a chip on her shoulder; to this day, she feels inferior to her older sister. Her older sister was full of charm, very popular. I was very close to her the last two years of her life. And out of that I came to the conclusion that we each had our character, but it alternated.
    Elizabeth—"Little Heart"—was a neglected child, not very smart but good-natured. My older one and younger sister were very

grasping: "Oh, you're going to give it to me!" One does it behind your back and the other one does it to your face. The older one would put a knife in your back. The older one is still around. She and myself are still sole survivors. I'm civil to her because I am civil to everybody. My Israeli wife tried to bring everybody together—family is very important to Israelis.

Ileana's second husband, Dr. Stefan Nikolaus Issarescu, was Romanian.

Another thing with my mother is she trusted everybody, at least if they were Romanian. Romanians could do no wrong. So she trusted this man and she married him. We disliked him. All of us. And I didn't say anything. My brother said he was the only one who could have said something, but she was so happy he didn't want to take that from her.

I was still picturing Ileana wearing salesgirl-style glasses with straps on the ears. That image seemed totally incongruent with the princess I had come to know through Carol Bacha.

And the second husband lived off my mother for five years. Because when he came to the states with her all his papers and stuff had been stolen. He was a pathologist—when they separated he said, "I don't even have my papers."

Dominic believes he was the cause of their divorce, though he maintains it would have occurred anyway.

We were in our house in Newton—I was the only child in the house at the time. It was my mother, her husband, and a man named George, an old family friend, a close friend to my brother's. And we were in the house and I had acute appendicitis. So they took me to the hospital. I don't remember how old I was; late teens, 20 actually. There was friction between my mother and her husband. And I don't know who started it. And here I was: he said that; she said that; then I said: "Why don't you say so-and-so?" By the end of the evening, the divorce was there. My brother Stefan didn't want the divorce to happen so soon. He wanted the pathologist to get his license to practice, so I sped it up. I didn't cause it, I sped it up. He moved out and remarried. I saw him before he died. His second wife asked me if I wanted some of his things, so some old family things I got back.

Dominic mentions a very beautiful miniature painting of his mother and grandmother.

He [Stefan] had it. He took a lot of letters from my mother that I have now. I have a diary of my mother's. And I know you want to ask me to let you read it. I'll tell you right now, I'm not even sure where it is. I don't think the diary would give you any insight. John F. Kennedy brought my mother into the country. He introduced a bill to let us immigrate to the United States.

I ask Dominic how many of Ileana's children are still Roman Catholic.

Mother tried to get me to convert to the Episcopal Church all my life. She felt I should become Episcopalian. I must admit that of all the Christian religions, it's the one that appeals to me the most. But I saw no reason to change. If you're a thinking person, you make up your own mind. Catholicism doesn't allow it ... to make up your own mind. Religion is a thing you write books about but you can't prove it, there's no real evidence. Why argue about it? I know I've been to St. Peter's Gate at least five times already and came back. People talk about shining lights and tunnels, but you know there's no proof. When I was a baby I almost drowned. Somebody at the swimming pool said, "Oh, Dominic is swimming at the bottom of the pool." My mother dove in and she brought me out.

I have arthritis, excruciating pain; I can go at any time. I've been to the monastery but I was the only one who was not at the funeral because I was in the Caribbean at the time. My mother was still in the trailer when I visited the monastery. I shared one of the houses on monastery property with my wife and stepdaughter. And I keep feeling I should go back, but it is such a long ride. It's eight hours to get there. I would do it for my mother for a visit, but for myself

I wouldn't do it. If it was three to four hours away I would go, but it is eight hours.

Ellwood City, Pennsylvania, is a very long trip from Philadelphia or New York. I told Dominic about my trip to Transfiguration and how complicated it can be to get from Pittsburgh to the monastery.

I don't know why she went there [Ellwood City]. The climate is horrible. My mother left all her literary things to the convent. It took a while to get it to the nuns in Pennsylvania because it went through many channels in Romania. I will probably take a diary I have of my mother's to the convent. It's a travel log diary.

Dominic says he left Romania with his family when he was nine years old.

The going from Romania to Switzerland to Argentina and then to Newton, Massachusetts, took me around the world. But nobody else did what I did. My brother eventually went to Detroit, and that was that. My sisters all went back to Austria, but I couldn't stand the prejudices there and my own marriage at the time was falling apart. So I decided I had to go somewhere that was neutral. So I went to the Caribbean [where he was exposed to a lot of sun, hence the trip to the dermatologist before he picked me up at Purdys station]. My sisters got married and all of them remained in Salzburg, Austria. I did go to Austria, and from there immediately started working all over the place—France, Italy.

I ask Dominic if he ever maintains contact with other European royals.

I didn't know what my name was until I was 13. Until then I was Dominic of Austria, then I became a Habsburg. At 13, I didn't understand, it didn't make any sense to me. I went back to Austria myself to meet various members of the Habsburg family, but after a few years I stopped going back to do this. You know, there's a Protestant and Italian line of Habsburgs as well as Catholic.

My meeting with Dominic took place months before he decided to sell Bran Castle. At that time he was experiencing considerable frustration at the way the castle was being presented to the public. I went to Bran Castle several months after our luncheon and found it to be the way he described it: "They made a museum out of it; we made the building a museum the way the family had it, but now it is partially family and partially a museum."

The castle is filled with narrow stone stairways that some tourists might find hard to navigate. In many instances it was necessary to duck your head or walk bent low so you would not hit the low ceilings. The labyrinth of corridors sometimes lead to indoor courtyards—the "ah" moment captured so succinctly in photo books or tourist postcards. The main lower rooms, or the family area Dominic referenced, include Queen Marie's breakfast table, where one easily spots a large wooden statue of Saint Joseph placed squarely in a niche.

King Ferdinand's bed and bedroom—the bed is a large canopied bed with royal trappings—recalled for me Dominic's comments about the royal couple's marriage; that Queen Marie, at 17, did not know what the hell she was doing when it came to lovemaking and that both of them had a number of love affairs. I also found it interesting when I visited the castle that a female guide was stationed by the door of the king's bedroom. Her role seemed to be information-based, but she was obviously also there for security purposes. One cannot have tourists lounging or napping on the king's bed for photo-ops.

Numerous photos and paintings of Ileana, Anton, and their children can be found throughout the place. Queen Marie's "presence" is also quite palpable. The upper floors of Bran Castle hit the visitor like cream pies thrown in Three Stooges movies. Suddenly we see mannequins of Dracula placed upside down in coffins, or those representing victims being tortured. Replica outfits and uniforms of what the real Dracula wore are neatly decked out on torso mannequins behind glass. The tackiness of it all hits you hard. The tourists I observed looking at this part of the exhibition seemed to soak it in quickly without comment; most of the people walking through the castle seemed to focus on the museum part. The souvenir shop on a lower floor offers all sorts of paraphernalia: handsome hardback editions of Bram Stoker's *Dracula*, coffee mugs, T-shirts, notebooks, refrigerator magnets, handbags, Queen

Marie's face on key chains, as well as copies of her memoirs and books written by Ileana.

Big, bold tour buses line the parking lot outside the castle. The lines of people emerging from these buses pass through an array of small rustic-looking shops that seem to sell everything from waffles to castle and Dracula memorabilia, although a large restaurant for the more sedate-minded is also available. But it is a long walk to the castle entrance itself, all uphill on authentic hard-on-your shoes big blocks of stone. With my guide, Constantine, I was able to bypass the congestion of ticket buyers at the castle's base, so up we went. It is one of those walks that might have kids asking, "When are we gonna get there?"

Prior to my visit to Bran, Dominic told me he was getting ready for a change in castle management.

"I've had to hire lawyers to get rid of lawyers," he said. "The lawyers I used to get the property back invested themselves so heavily in the project that now I have to fight to get them out." These lawyers are American, because Dominic thought American lawyers would keep the Romanians honest. "But no!" he says. "The Americans are terrible. They exploited us. All of this is nerve-wracking. I'm not built for this. I stand up for my rights but I don't go on about lost causes."

The waitress brings us an ice cream dessert. Instead of individual servings—chocolate for Dominic and vanilla for me—she delivers one common bowl containing both scoops and swirls of whipped cream. She blames the shared bowl on the ice-cream scooper in the kitchen. We share the dessert as Dominic reminisces about living in Venice for ten years. I relate a story I heard years ago about the canals in Venice stinking because they are filled with human waste, and the time a young Katherine Hepburn dove into them for a swim and came out with a life-altering health condition.

"Well, the canals that do smell are called 'dead arms,'" Dominic says. The prince sitting before me adds that living in Newton, Massachusetts, was fun:

I basically have no childhood friends. In Romania it was school all day and then weekends with siblings. There were some friends ... but hardly any children's time.

I haven't been to Bran in five years. It now takes four hours to travel to Bran by car from Bucharest when it should only take two. That's because of the traffic. As I told you, I had a criminal case against the Bran lawyers. Romanians are not known for their honesty. I have no prejudices myself, except gypsies. Stealing is a part of their trade, their culture.

We finish up our ice cream as Dominic checks the time because I am scheduled to take the train from Purdys back to the city. But there is just one more story to tell.

I was on a ship with a friend of mine from New York to Germany. And I met a witch. She said she was a witch. There were young kids on the boat; the whole thing was fun. Then she said she was a Druid. And she said: "I was watching you. You don't move around at all. But you miss nothing." And in a way she's right, I am an observer. I don't have to partake. She was funny, she was huge. I was dancing with her. I was holding on for dear life. I'm dancing with a barrel and she thought it the funniest thing she ever heard. She remains my friend to this day.

10

Romania Today

Fascism, Nazism, Communism and Socialism are only superficial variations of the same monstrous theme—collectivism.

—Ayn Rand

As a seasoned travel journalist, I almost canceled my trip to Romania several times before finally opting to go. I was not sure why I was feeling fearful. The rash of plane crashes across the globe did not help, but then I realized that most of these crashes involved small, private planes, while I would be traveling on a British Airways jumbo jet.

Why Romania and not Italy, Paris, or Rome? Working on this book about the life and influence of Princess Ileana of Romania suggested the need to touch Romanian soil and experience the people living there.

And so I flew to London, and after a brief layover I took a flight to Bucharest, capital of Romania. I had never been to London's Heathrow Airport before, so I was not prepared for the nightmare that awaited me. Heathrow is so large that a half-hour bus ride is necessary to reach some of the gates. My impression of London through the Heathrow lens was not good. I thought I was in Constantinople or in another Middle Eastern country. Practically the only white Europeans I saw were faded billboard images of the late Queen Elizabeth II. In any event, I was glad to be on the Romania-bound plane, even if it was a small jet and subject to mountain turbulence, and even if I was seated in the last seat closest to the bathroom so that by the time we landed I knew every passenger's bathroom habits.

Romanian Customs threw me into a mental tailspin. The crowds of people from arrival flights moved in a large confusing mass towards the Customs officials. Unlike most ports of entry, this crowd was left to its own devices when it came to forming orderly lines. When a sense of decorum did eventually emerge, I found myself face-to-face with a thin, severe-looking bureaucrat who looked at me as if trying to discern an ulterior motive for entering the country. After asking where I was from, he paused for a few seconds, looked into my eyes, then raised his passport stamp high in the air and let it come crashing down with a roaring "thud!"

Among the people cramming Customs were several migrant types in West African garb. I noticed some Romanians in the crowd giving them disapproving looks. I had read that many Romanians are fed up with the immigration policies as advocated by the EU. (Romania joined the EU in 2007.)

My guide for a four-day road trip through the western and northern parts of the country, Constantine—an ice hockey player who dabbles in art history—drove me to the Hotel Berthelot, where we arranged to meet the following morning for the beginning of our journey.

In the hotel parking lot, Constantine pointed out a couple of vehicles with Ukraine license plates. "These are Ukrainian migrants escaping the war," he said. "They come to Romania, where they stay for free at hotels and eat for free in the dining rooms. After that they are fitted for free housing."

Constantine said the program was EU-based and discriminatory to poor Romanians, who have no such privileges.

Upon investigating this matter later, I discovered that the UN's Refugee Agency (UNHCR) states:

Refugees from Ukraine who enter Romania for the first time since the start of the conflict, starting from 1 July 2024, have the right to accommodation assistance in temporary and humanitarian accommodation centres. Alternatively, eligible refugees can receive a lump sum for a maximum of three consecutive months, amounting to 750 RON/month for a single person and 2000 RON/month for a family. [RON has been the Romanian currency code and foreign exchange symbol since 2005.]

My first night in Bucharest was not good. I felt out of sync and wanted to return to Philadelphia. I thought a walk through Bucharest might be a good idea, but once outside on city streets I could not muster the enthusiasm to visit a café. Jet lag was kicking in. I was caught off-guard when a girl (in her twenties) ran up to me on the sidewalk, presented me with a business card, and asked if I wanted a massage. Did I look that lonely?

Constantine met me the following morning. He was dressed in a spiffy, jockey-like jacket that had the word "Romania" printed in large block letters on the back. He brought snacks and drinks from a little general store he owned. We started our drive on Route 130, a road he said was designed by Hitler and that went all the way to Russia.

It is true that road-building was a high priority under the Hitler government. Immediately after taking office, the regime introduced subsidies for car ownership. After that, a German company was formed to build the world's first nationwide highway system.

Before heading out on Hitler's road, Constantine pointed out a neoclassical-style building that used to serve as a headquarters for the Gestapo and the German Embassy (prior to 1944), when Hitler's puppet dictator, Ion Antonescu, controlled the country. Nazi rule in Romania ended in 1944 when Romania's King Michael, at the tender age of 22, successfully forced out Antonescu, saving thousands of Jews from extermination. Antonescu previously had been given a free hand by Hitler to solve the "Jewish question," which resulted in the murder of at least 420,000 Jews early in the war. Ironically, Antonescu's Nazi regime was followed by an even harsher communist one.

Constantine talked about the Bucharest restaurant his grandparents owned during World War Two:

> The Nazis would come in, say hello, order food, leave a big tip, say thank you and then leave. When the communists took over, they came into the restaurant, smashed the liquor cabinets, drank all the alcohol, ate their meals without paying, and threatened to rape my grandmother.

Our first road stop was an outdoor barbecue sausage stand staffed by middle-aged women in headscarves. Constantine said it was a popular "truck" stop on the way to Transylvania and beyond. The women tended to sizzling sausages of various sizes as small gypsy children wandered the area asking for money. A boy of 6 or 7 walked up to our table with his hand out; he was later joined by his younger sister. An old gypsy woman, talking to unseen spirits, paced back and forth near where we were eating. Constantine inferred that the women at the grill also offered "other" services if one was interested. It was hard for me to wrap my mind around this because they looked like the good Orthodox Christians one sees bowing and crossing themselves before church icons.

We drove through the Olt River gorge and valley and stopped at the Cozia Monastery, built in 1388. To my surprise, my guide purchased a bottle of holy oil from Mount Athos in the small gift shop there and made a show of anointing my forehead, lips, and hands with the oil in the middle of the church.

Romania's political history is a study in subservience. The country fell to Ottoman suzerainty in 1541; its liberation from Ottoman rule occurred in 1871. After the Turks were driven out of the country by the Hapsburg Austrian emperor, there was an Austrian push to convert Orthodox Christians to Catholicism.

Many Orthodox monasteries and churches were confiscated and used as horse stables. Two notable Orthodox churches—Voroneţ Monastery, which we would visit later, founded and erected by Stephen the Great in 1488, and the Cozia Monastery church, built in 1388 by Mircea the Elder, grandfather of Vlad Dracula—became hovels for a variety of barnyard animals. Constantine blamed the conversion of the Cozia Monastery church into a stable on the Austrian Jesuits.

Near the Cozia church, an elderly gypsy man sold us a pair of hand-sculpted wooden tomahawks for two American dollars.

We entered the town of Sibiu before heading to Timişoara, where Lenten worshippers crowded the immense 300ft-tall Metropolitan Orthodox Cathedral with its mosaic-patterned roof tiles. We walked through Victory Square, the seat of the 1989 Romanian Revolution that overthrew the communist Ceauşescu dictatorship.

At a café there, we asked if they sold real American coffee, an almost impossible acquisition in most of Romania as espresso and its infinite varieties dominate every gas station rest stop and restaurant. When Constantine asked the proprietor, he said "yes" but what he presented were large cups filled with a kind of watered-down espresso. The local McDonald's seemed promising in this regard, but even there watered-down espresso in a large cup was presented as "American."

Sneakers are a hot item in Romania. A large sneaker store in Victory Square was buzzing with large crowds and numerous security guards. Immediately after entering the shop, we were followed by a young female employee who watched as Constantine found some sneakers he liked. He asked if the marked price of 50 Euros for them was correct, but was told by the employee they were really 150 Euros and that the labeling was a mistake.

"This trickery happens all the time in Romania," he said. "The list price is never the real price."

Bram Stoker, who wrote the notes for his gothic novel *Dracula* in Philadelphia when he visited in 1884 (he completed the work in Scotland in 1896), never traveled to Romania. However, he did research the country and knew its mystical traditions and folklore. These include tales of giants that protected the Earth and wizards descended from Dacians (Dacia being the former name of Romania).

When we traveled through Transylvania, Constantine pointed out that many Romanians still observe the old custom of driving a stake through the heart of the deceased, as well as keeping the body at home for at least three days for mourning and prayers. A glass of water and a piece of bread are generally placed before the body during this period so that the spirit may partake before its journey into the afterlife.

Constantine told me he has witnessed the water in these glasses disappear slowly without being touched by human hands. Deceased relatives are sometimes buried on family property rather than in cemeteries. When we crossed the Carpathian Mountains, a mild April snowstorm was in progress. He talked about the myth of the wolfmen who inhabit the forests here. What is no myth are brown bears that sometimes kill humans. When he stopped the car so he could take a smoke, he mentioned attacks by Eurasian lynx which appear suddenly from behind trees and will attack and gnaw at your ankles.

Nearly 75 percent of Romanians belong to the Romanian Orthodox Church, while 6 percent are Protestant and 4 percent Roman or Greek Catholic. Along the highways and small roads, Orthodox crucifix mosaic shrines are as numerous as trees. Small chapels and churches are everywhere. In a shopping mall parking lot, I noticed a very small golden-domed chapel next to a fast-food outlet. The farther north you go—at one point we were forty minutes from the Ukraine border—the more Protestant (Lutheran) churches there are. German influence, especially Bavarian architecture, is common in towns like Brasov and Gura Humorului.

I planned my trip in December 2024 about the time Romania's Constitutional Court canceled the results of the presidential election in which conservative Călin Georgescu won the popular vote on the first round of voting. Georgescu's victory created panic among status quo pro-EU liberal politicians, causing the liberal judiciary to claim that Russia had somehow influenced the election results. The Russian interference claim was never proven, just as it was never proven—and later disproven—when Hilary Clinton made the same claim about her 2016 election defeat to Donald Trump in the United States.

The judiciary, so it seems, is an enemy of true democracy in Romania, just as it has recently been proven to be the enemy of democracy in the United States, with the "law-fare" attacks through the courts on Donald Trump to try to halt his second run for the presidency.

Rod Dreher had some interesting things to say on his blog *Rod Dreher's Diary* about the suppression of Romania's 2024 election results:

Bear in mind that I'm not on the ground in Romania; I'm just repeating to you what my friends and contacts there are telling me about all this—things I'm not seeing in the Western media, and probably will not. A couple of weeks ago, the great Romanian pundit Titus Techera, who now lives in Budapest, was explaining to me the appeal of Georgescu. It was really, really interesting. What I recall mostly from that conversation was his saying that Georgescu really is deeply in touch with the mainstream of Romanian society—a very conservative culture whose members, like the faithful Orthodox who came to hear me speak that afternoon in Bucharest, have been told for years by the political establishment to shut up and be ashamed of themselves, and let the pro-Brussels, pro-Washington elites run things, because everyone will be better off.

The Romanian people don't buy it anymore. Their governing elites might be ashamed to be Romanian, and to stand for Romanian interests, but most voters no longer are. That's why they voted Georgescu in the first round. And that's why he was set to win a landslide this weekend, until the Deep State intervened.

Remember, in Europe, democracy is when people vote the way Brussels wants them to. And as we learned with our own Russiagate pseudo-scandal, always look to the butthurt establishment to cite supposed threats from Russia as a reason to negate or otherwise discredit the outcome of a democratic election.

Gheorghe Gheorghieu-Dej, leader of the Romanian Communist Party, became the nation's first communist leader. He served until 1965 and was followed by Nicolae Ceaușescu, a dictator who held the reins of power until 1989, when communism began to fall throughout Eastern Europe. (The execution by firing squad of Ceaușescu and his wife, Elena, officially marked the end of communist rule.)

My Romanian guide announced that he admired President Trump and told me he hoped his country follows America's lead and elects a Trump-like nationalist in the May 4 and May 18, 2025 national elections. Throughout much of our journey, he expounded on the current state of affairs in the country.

He told me that while most Romanians dislike Russia, they have an even greater contempt for Ukraine, a country which he called brutish and insensitive. "If I were to drive us across the border into Ukraine, we wouldn't last long. We would be 'disappeared,'" he said.

Fortunately, a tour of Ukraine was not on the agenda. When we passed a car with a Ukraine license plate, he remarked how Ukrainians like to escape the bleakness of their country by taking car trips into Romania's scenic Carpathian Mountain region. "Their country is so bleak and gray, they need Romanian beauty," he said.

When we drove through the countryside, we passed large abandoned factories built during the communist era. These buildings reflect the ugliness and barrenness of communism. They sit like dark monoliths in an otherwise beautiful terrain. Some of these abandoned factories are twenty stories tall, with eerily small windows reminiscent of prisons. Even in Bucharest, once known as the Paris of the East, one can see many large-scale communist buildings, some of them now falling apart and rotting.

Even if one knew nothing about communist ideology and how it works, the bounty of leftover ugly communist architecture all over Romania stands as a testament as to why a country should never go communist.

Bran Castle, once owned by the Romanian royal family and cherished as a favorite family residence by Queen Marie, was robbed of most of its furniture by the Stalinist reformers, who wanted to destroy all traces of royalty. A few authentic pieces of furniture managed to escape the plunder, such as Queen Marie's breakfast table and the bed of King Ferdinand, but for the most part what visitors see are replica replacements.

The castle, as previously noted, is filled with tacky Vlad Dracula paraphernalia, the most shocking being a Dracula dummy placed upside down in a coffin, installed by boardwalk commercialists in a bid to attract tourists. (For the record, Vlad Dracula never set foot in Bran Castle.)

Although Romania joined the European Union in 2007, many Romanians are now questioning that alliance. Currently, under the direction of the EU, the country is undergoing an expansive road-building explosion which is causing multiple traffic detours in and out of Bucharest.

"Why the need to build new highways?" Constantine asked as we drove through the Olt River gorge. "The roads we have are fine. They just need repaving. All this construction is not necessary." On numerous occasions we were stuck in long lines of traffic with scores of trucks, unwieldy detours that went on for miles and miles.

An even bigger issue for Romanians in the May 2025 elections was immigration.

While driving down one of Bucharest's main thoroughfares, he pointed out Turkish and Middle Eastern immigrants hanging out in the streets in groups of five or ten. "They do nothing all day long. They gather in groups and do nothing—nothing. It gets worse all the time."

The National Salvation Front (FSN) was the first post-communist political party established in Romania. In 1993, the FSN split into two parties, the largest being the Social Democratic Party (PSD), a leftist mirror image of the Democrat Party in the United States. When I visited the country, the Romanian Prime Minister, Ion Marcel Ciolacu, has been the leader of the PSD since 2019, and much like his leftist cohorts in the Social Liberal Humanist Party, was likely to label anyone who challenged the EU and its policies a "right-wing extremist."

In April 2025, Romanian polls had former PSD leftist-turned-conservative, Victor Ponta, running for president as an independent, coming second in the first election round after conservative nationalist George Simion, who was considered the favorite. With two conservatives in the lead, it seemed likely that Romania would get its own Donald Trump.

Yet Romania's top court was quite active in barring nationalist politicians like Diana Șoșoacă from 2025's and the annulled 2024 presidential election. Șoșoacă might be called Romania's Marine Le Pen. Ruthless in her comments, she once said, "The EU and NATO destroy everything they touch … Europe is corrupt from the very tip. Serbians are the bravest people in all of Europe. Most Serbians do not wish to be part of the EU because they've seen what happened to Romania and to what extent Romania has been destroyed."

Other candidates in the May 4 runoff included pro-EU Bucharest mayor Nicușor Dan, a member of the liberal USR party, and Elena Lasconi, a former journalist and the leader of the Save Romania Union Party.

The American publication *Politico* had this to say about the Romanian elections:

The Eastern European country of 19 million people borders Ukraine and is one of NATO's key eastern flank members, with access to the Black Sea. A victory by a far-right candidate in the presidential election threatens to bring Bucharest more in line with U.S. President

Donald Trump's MAGA movement while harming EU plans to continue aiding Ukraine in its defense against Russia's full-scale invasion.

That seemed to be the way things were going on May 4 when George Simion won the first round of the presidential election. Simion came first with 40.96 percent of the vote, and went into the runoff on May 18 as the clear favorite against the liberal mayor of Bucharest. But on Sunday May 18 (Sunday Bloody Sunday!), Nicușor Dan, the centrist pro-EU candidate, managed to squeak to victory.

Appendix I

Alexei Lives: The Harry Binkow Files

A constant theme during my interviews with Bacha/Mother Elizabeth was her assertion that some members of the Russian royal family survived the execution by Bolshevik revolutionaries on the night of July 16/17, 1918, in Ekaterinburg, Russia. Although this version of events contradicts the official version now standard in most history books, serious questions were later raised by historians such as Harry Binkow, who knew Bacha and communicated with her for a number of years. Ileana's own views on this topic were often expressed to Bacha; these views mostly aligned with Binkow's "re-reading" of the execution story. The inclusion of the "Harry Binkow Files" in the Appendices, as well as data from an examination of the skulls from the Ekaterinburg remains, and an interview with Alexei Romanov in 1966, will hopefully give the reader an alternative historical insight into what happened to the Russian royal family.

The historian Harry Binkow wrote in 2019/2020:

Members of the Romanov royal family survived? What is wrong with the official version of the events of July 1918?

Unbelievable, but true: the official version of the murder of the imperial Romanov family literally bursts at the seams. More and more professional historians have begun to declare its failure.

In particular, the historian Nikolai Sapelkin, in one of his last programs on the Day TV channel, said that when clarifying the circumstances of the death of the imperial family and some other Romanovs, many inaccuracies were revealed. First of all, by shooting:

"In the small basement of the Ipatiev House it was impossible to shoot members of the royal family with the firing squad and according to the script that Yurovsky prescribed [speech about a brochure/note by Yurovsky, commandant of the Ipatiev House].

Yes, now, with the efforts of Andropov and Yeltsin, the house is destroyed, there is no basement. You can't put an investigative experiment, but there are measurements of it, and when they try to build a model, nothing looms."

Even more details about the place of the alleged execution of the royal family can be found in the story of the historian Yuri Zhukov: "The room where they were supposed to be shot, ~ 20 square meters and a height of 1.75 meters. ... Put 22 people in this 20-meter room. They will stand close. How to shoot?"

What is interesting: according to Zhukov, only one spot resembling blood was found in the basement. "12 people were shot," he is amazed, "well, there must be at least 12 drops of blood!" "Next," he continues. "They shot many times, but on the walls they found only three who were kicked out of bullets."

An interesting nuance: Zhukov claims that his beard and mustache were found shaved in the rooms of Nicholas II. In the girls' room they found cut braids. All this was found on the first day that the Czechs entered Ekaterinburg.

As for the bodies: "all investigators, while many of them are professional and judicial investigators of the tsarist era," Zhukov said, "were looking for traces. They didn't find anything. Well, no trace of the bodies. Not! Then it was suggested that they were shot, taken out, burned, and that which did not burn, was doused with hydrochloric acid. Everything dissolved. "Therefore, there are no bodies."

An important nuance: according to Zhukov, the version of the execution of the imperial family is mainly based on the brochure of Yurovsky. "But this pamphlet," he says, "was written not by Yurovsky, but by the famous historian of the left-radical views of Pokrovsky. What for? But very simple: the absence of corpses was unprofitable for us. Why? "Since they are not there, it means that somewhere there is a living Nicholas II and it can be made a banner of the counter-revolution and anything else."

As you know, the remains of the Romanov family were "officially found" in 1991. In fact, they were found in the summer of 1979 in the Porosenkov ravine near Ekaterinburg by the screenwriter G. Ryabov and the Sverdlovsk local historian A. Avdonin.

Yuri Zhukov is convinced that the discovery of the remains is falsification. He argues his opinion as follows: "Suddenly, the man who became famous for his film, he wrote the text 'Born of the Revolution' about the workers and peasants' militia [G. Ryabov], he goes, digs and takes out. Sorry, but in life this does not happen. They explain: a geologist allegedly helped him. A geologist can look for oil, copper ore, etc., but not the remains that are about 75 years old.

"Archaeologists or forensic scientists who know how to look for old graves are looking for such things." "Moreover, after such a period it is simply impossible to find—it is impossible," the historian sums up.

... So, we come to 1991. We supposedly slip the remains. To clarify whose they are, a genetic examination is needed. In the world in Europe there is one of the best laboratories in Leipzig at the Planck Institute of the German Academy of Sciences. They were ready to conduct a study there, but said: "It will take us 2-3 years to be sure."

We urgently send the remains to Florida, where, to whom—is unknown. Well, there are no such centers there. Nevertheless, we get confirmation from them: "Yes, everything is in order." What you wanted is what you got.

So what happened to the Romanovs? Could they survive?

The historian Nikolai Sapelkin claims that the Soviet government did not plan to kill the king. "It is known," he says, that Lenin wanted to judge the king [following the example of Louis XVI]. Show everyone which worthless person ruled the state. Sentencing the king to labor, either a janitor or a lumberjack. "There were thoughts of exchanging him for leaders of the international revolutionary movement: Karl Liebknecht and Rosa Luxemburg."

A curious story in this regard is told by the historian Yuri Zhukov with reference to a certain English historian whom he met more than 20 years ago during a conference in Cambridge.

"While working in 1986-1987 on a book on the foreign policy of the German Empire during the First World War, this historian delved into the German archives and accidentally found correspondence between Berlin and Moscow about the exchange of Nicholas II and his wife for K. Liebknecht and R. Luxemburg."

"The correspondence referred to the end of September — October," Zhukov said. "It was clear from it that both sides were looking for a suitable place where these people could be exchanged." And then suddenly everything is interrupted. In Germany—a revolution. "The correspondence is ending."

"But this is curious," emphasizes Zhukov, "if you try to find it in encyclopedias, reference books, when you released Liebknecht from prison, you will not find this. For one simple reason: he was released two weeks before the revolution—October 20, 1918. Why? In honor of what? "I can't say exactly what happened there."

"I know one thing," Zhukov summarizes, "in our archives there are no documents about the so-called execution of the royal family. They are absent."

"I suppose," said the historian, "that the Romanovs were sent there, to the West, to Germany. Moreover, we well know that they had a huge amount of money in an English bank, but we forget that millions of Romanov gold were also in Berlin.

"Therefore, all of them could exist comfortably without manifesting themselves."

A piquant nuance: according to another historian Sergei Ivanovich [the tsarist historian] in the KGB of the USSR there was a department for monitoring all movements of members of the tsarist family. It was abolished only in 1991 [recall that in the same year the remains of the Romanovs were found "miraculously"].

The department's archive was sent to the Urals. "Actually, if you wish," says Ivanovich, "you can always return this archive and show people the truth: how this department worked for decades, how they watched all the Romanov's relatives who lived on the territory of the USSR."

Interesting evidence: the historian Ivanovich claims that the two daughters of Nicholas II, Tatiana and Anastasia, had children, [and] his son Alexei also had them. [dzen.ru/a/XH63PZArhwCyyO4j?fbc lid=IwARobD5ZvA5HBcayEWAHl3D-Yt9k8guxAQpbRQVWkYX UmTRlZkkdzyHAPxQE]

The following is Harry Binkow's review of *The Escape of Alexei, Son of Tsar Nicholas II* by Vadim Petrov, Igor Lysenho, and Georgy Egorov (1998, Harry N. Abrams, Inc., New York):

May 22, 2018

These men did nothing to research Alexei. They are way off topic with this character. I am the only one that has confirmed Alexei's existence with facts and documented evidence. Tsarevich Alexei Nicholaevich Romanov was retrieved from Yalta, on the Crimean Peninsula with his Aunt Elizabeth Feodorovna, aboard the HMS *Marlborough*, with his grandmother, Dowager Empress Marie Feodorovna. Both escorted to the Captain's quarters, one a lovely elder lady, the other a much younger lady ...

In 1916, Lord Charles Hardinge returned to his former post in England as Permanent Under-Secretary at the Foreign Office, serving with Arthur Balfour. In 1920 he became ambassador to France before his retirement in 1922.

In April 1919, Lord Charles Hardinge, 1st Baron Hardinge, received Penshurst's letter. Binkow wrote,

There is final irony about the Lord Hardinge's letter and its role in solving the case. The letter most definitely seems to have been provoked by the coming to England of Nicholas's mother, the one figure whose dichotomous accounts of her son's family maintained to the date of her death—but always off-the record—that none were assassinated.

She left strong clues all along her rout: on the battleship *Marlborough* which picked her up at Yalta, at Malta, where she way gay and the life of all parties held for her, and aboard the battleship *Lord Nelson* which carried her on the final stage of her trip to England.

After most of them were aboard, I noticed our Captain B. S. Thesiger stop ashore in order to escort a wonderful-looking elder lady (Ella) and younger companion (Alexei in female clothing). These two were taken by him to his cabin, but because we all had our hands full getting the other ladies bedded down, and then going back to sea, I did not get a close look at the ladies who spent the night in the Captain's quarters.

The next morning the Captain Thesiger, who had slept in an auxiliary cabin, told me where his quarters would be for a few days because, as his messenger, I had to be within easy call. He also told me that the elder lady (Ella) in his cabin was none other than Grand Duchess Feodorovna, and the younger one accompanying her the Prince Royal Alexei, whom I had escorted on the visit to our ship.

Applying the British terms "Princess Royal" to the Russian Court where it was not used, but as Captain Thesiger probably understood it, it would have meant the senior of the Tsar's four daughters, the Grand Duchess Olga. In 1919 she would have been 24. But only the Grand Duchess Marie, born in 1890, and the Grand Duchess Anastasia, born in 1901, could reasonably have fitted Limbrick's description of being about his own age (17) at the time.

These persons in the orbit of the Imperial Family had the name "Feodorovna" associated with them. They were Nicholas II's mother, Dowager Empress Marie Feodorovna, whose trip to England on the HMS *Marlborough* and *Lord Nelson* we have already traced, and the two German-born sisters, Empress Alexandra Feodorovna, Nicholas's wife, and Elizabeth, Grand Duchess, both of whom [were] reportedly slain by the Reds before [their ship] *Calypso* ever reached the Black Sea. Both had adopted "Feodorovna" to follow the first names so that the Tsarina called herself "Alexandra Feodorovna," and her sister, "Elizabeth Feodorovna."

The ship took Dowager Empress Maria Feodorovna and other members of the former, deposed Russian Imperial Family including Grand Duke Nicholas and Prince Felix Yusupov aboard in Yalta on the evening of the 7th. The Empress refused to leave unless the British also evacuated wounded and sick soldiers, along with any civilians that also wanted to escape the advancing Bolsheviks. The Russian entourage aboard *Marlborough* numbered some 80 people, including 44 members of the Royal Family and nobility, with a number of governesses, nurses, maids and man servants, plus several hundred cases of luggage.

An Interview with Alexei Romanov in 1966

During my research into the supposed death of Alexei Romanov, Mother Elizabeth (Bacha) sent me a faded 1966 publication called *Richard Cotten's Conservative Viewpoint*. This weekly bulletin was published in Bakersfield, California, and served to publish transcripts of Cotten's daily fifteen-minute radio interviews. Labeled "Script Number 163-166 Broadcast on July 11-14, 1966," the interview was simply titled, "Aleksei Nicholaevich Romanoff." Cotten asserts that Alexei was not killed in 1918 with other members of the Russian royal family, but in fact survived and adopted a new name, Colonel Michael Goleniewski.

Cotten begins: "You may recall that we brought you what I thought to be valuable information some months ago relative to the strange case of Aleksei Nikolaevich Romanoff [why Cotten uses this strange spelling is never explained], the son of Czar Nicholas II, the last of the Russian Czars.

"This transcript will deal with an interview which I recently had in New York with Aleksei Nikolaevich Romanoff, Mr. Herman E. Kimsey who was formerly associated with the C.I.A., and expert Cleve Backster. The interview with these gentlemen began as follows:"

Mr. Cotten: I believe it might have merit if we found a simpler way of expressing your name for the purpose of this interview, as your official title is: His Imperial Highness, the Heir to the All-Russian Imperial Throne, Tsarevich and Grand Duke Aleksei Nikolaevich of Russia and August Ataman-Knight of Orders: Of St. Andrew, St. Aleksandr Nevski, St. George, St. Nicholas of Seraphins of Sweden, Legion D'Honneur, etc.

Mr. Romanoff: If you please, Sir, you may address me as Mr. Romanoff.

Mr. Cotten: Then I will be pleased to do so. Another gentleman who is to be included in this interview is Mr. Cleve Backster and he is with the Polygraph Research Committee of the Academy for Scientific Interrogation. You will see that Mr. Backster had an important part to play in the establishment of the identity of this sister of Aleksei Romanoff, who was Anastasia Nikolaevna, the Grand Duchess of Russia a/k/a Eugenia Smith. The third person included in this interview is Mr. H. E. Kinsey, a former official of the Central Intelligence Agency, who has personal knowledge that the C.I.A. has information in their possession which would, beyond any doubt, establish the proper identity of the man known to our Government as Colonel Goleniewski. I wonder if at this point it would not be wise to refer to the *Herald of Freedom* [article] of February 11, 1966 and March 25, 1966 entitled "The Strange Case of Col. Goleniewski," which was developed by Frank Capell, and ask if, in your opinion, Mr. Romanoff, you find these facts about yourself to be true and accurate.

Mr. Romanoff: Yes, Sir, I can state that the contents of the two issues of the *Herald of Freedom* by Frank Capell regarding my real identity and my voluntary support for the national security of the United States and other areas mentioned in these two issues are truthful and correct.

Mr. Cotten: Thank you, Sir! As we develop this, I, too, feel that America must have this information and we will do all that we can to compile it in this transcript, making it understandable and concise. We will also reproduce information from the *Herald of Freedom* and other pertinent documentation. Mr. Backster, would you at this time give us some information regarding the facts you have established concerning the Romanoffs?

Mr. Backster: My entry into the Romanoff case, or the "Reappearance of the Romanoffs" as we have captioned the case, started with an account of a client of mine in the Polygraph business brining to me an account or a story of an individual who stated that she was a close friend of Anastasia, the youngest daughter of Czar Nicholas II, who was not represented as being initially alive, but then later was actually admitted as being alive because of discrepancies that were found in the initial story of this woman and she was then tested on the Polygraph (or the so-called Lie Detector) regarding her identity. As a result of these tests, there was no doubt in my mind (as the Polygraph expert involved), and no doubt in the minds of individuals with whom I shared these charts, that this person was indeed the real Anastasia. To be quite certain that we were not making a mistake, as far as dealing with a delusional individual, we had this person, Eugenia Smith, (as she called herself at that time) attend four interviews with one of the top psychiatrists in the country who has dealt, and is dealing with missing persons and amnesia cases and things of that nature. The psychiatrist stated that there were no traces of a delusional personality and [with] this, combined with the Polygraph examination results, we felt certain of one thing—this was indeed Anastasia, the youngest daughter of Czar Nicholas II, despite all of the alleged evidence that was compiled saying otherwise.

Mr. Cotten: Now, how does this become pertinent, if you please, to the identity of Mr. Romanoff as we will be seeing?

Mr. Backster: This becomes quite pertinent because of a book that was published by Robert Speller & Sons in 1963. This book attracted the attention of an individual who visited the offices of the publisher and stated that he would like to meet this woman. This person stated that he was Aleksei Romanoff.

Mr. Cotten: Subsequent to that, the testimony I have seen substantiates that there was a confrontation between these two persons. Mr. Backster, could you tell us what developed?

Mr. Backster: Yes indeed! On December 31, 1963, these two individuals were introduced to each other as far as physical presence is concerned, without any prejudice as to identity, and the conversation was tape-recorded with the consent and knowledge of Anastasia (or Eugenia Smith as she was called then); the tape, indeed, was quite interesting and revealing.

Mr. Cotten: Did she recognize Aleksei as her brother?

Mr. Backster: She certainly did, and it was quite an emotional scene.

Mr. Cotten: In your opinion and your business, is it fully authenticated? Do you accept it at face value?

Mr. Backster: As far as the tape being authentic I can state this—that I did the tape recording so I can authenticate its existence—and the details surrounding this before, during and after this confrontation had been fully proven to the complete satisfaction of many individuals that this person is indeed Anastasia.

Mr. Cotten: First, we have proof that she is Anastasia and, through her, the proof that this is her brother.

Mr. Backster: Actually, the brother and the proof regarding his identity are separate issues that were confirmed in quite another channel and by another means, but the two do dovetail and agree.

Mr. Cotten: Might I say this? We have an audience, by and large, of the opinion that the entire family was murdered many, many years ago. We are now telling this audience that there is not only a daughter living, but also a son of a Czar. Since we will go into this a little later, can you give us a few words as to what has been developed to show that this execution simply did not take place?

Mr. Backster: In the examination of the evidence, in my capacity as coordinator of the investigation of the return of the Romanoffs, the careful study of the circumstances reported to have taken place or existed during the time of the alleged murder were based on their own merits, not accurate from a scientific standpoint. There were many other indications that came to light, even published data in newspapers as the *New York Times*, the *New York Tribune*, etc., stating after the alleged murder of the family that the family was indeed alive!

Mr. Cotten: I certainly wish to thank you. At this point, Mr. Romanoff, would you care to comment on what we had just had from Mr. Backster?

Mr. Romanoff: I am of the opinion that the statement of Mr. Cleve Backster is correct. It is true that I met my sister, Anastasia Nikolaevna on December 31st, 1963 at the office of her publisher, Robert Speller, in New York City, and at this time took place a mutual recognition between us which was tape recorded and which appears also as a separate statement of said publishing firm, Robert

Speller & Sons, Inc. I met Anastasia Nikolaevna, my sister, the first time here in the United States. She arrived or respectively immigrated to the United States in 1922. Since 1922 I had not seen her. I met her for the first time in 1963 in New York City. From the point of investigation of Mr. Backster and his Academy, there is no question that she is the real person, the Grand Duchess of Russia, Anastasia Nikolaevna. I believe that certain high officials in the United States Government were informed a long time ago about her real identity; there is no question about this fact today, and we have the publication of her autobiography which is not in all parts truthful. I had the opportunity to meet her because during this time between 1961, after I arrived in the United States and supplied competent officials of the C.I.A. and F.B.I. with data regarding my sister in the United States, for reasons beyond my control I couldn't see my sister up until December 31, 1963.

Mr. Cotten: Thank you, Mr. Romanoff, for this information. I would like to give you a little background on Mr. Herman E. Kimsey. From 1946 to 1953 he was a Special Agent of the U.S. Army Counter Intelligence Corps—this is the C.I.C. [From] 1953 to 1963 he was Section Chief and Officer for the United States Central Intelligence Agency. In 1964 he was Assistant Chief of Security including [the] Presidential Campaign of the Republican National Committee. In 1964 he was Security Consultant, Security Associate in Bethesda, Maryland. Mr. Herman Kimsey has an affidavit that will be photo-reproduced with this transcript and which will be much more meaningful with this interview with Mr. Kimsey. Mr. Kimsey, it is my understanding that the affidavit develops the fact that the C.I.A. has in its files the documentation needed to establish the identity of the man whom our Government knew for so long as "Col. Goleniewski" actually is that of Aleksei Nikolaevich. Could you give us some information on this?

Mr. Kimsey: Yes, Mr. Cotten! This information which you have just mentioned and which is in the files of the C.I.A. was brought to my attention some time ago. Then early in the stages of this investigation, after my severance of relationship with the C.I.A. in 1962, I became interested in this case through the intercession on the part of an old C.I.A. Agent friend of mine, Mr. Backster, who felt there was a development phase of this case which was not within the realm of his technical capacities and which I believe you have dismissed in a previous interview. He had asked me to intercede, considering the fact that my background was particularly directed around identification techniques, including personal identification.

Mr. Cotten: Then you will be developing your finger-print impressions, sole prints, dental charts, measurements, face prints, blood tests and, in other words, many, many various facets all to complete the identification. Is that correct?

Mr. Kimsey: Yes, that is correct. I might add while we are talking about these particular techniques, as a group they are rather interesting, I would imagine, to a layman, in the sense that they are primarily techniques which have not been exercised widely by Police Departments for approximately fifty years. Going back, by deduction alone, without going into the actual facts of the possession of these comparative materials on hand in the C.I.A. files, this takes us back to a period of time when the initial material was collected from all members of the Russian Imperial Family for the purpose of possible future identification and placed on deposit in the files of other countries. At this particular period of time they were using precisely some of the methods and techniques described by you, known as the Anthropometrical Test, which goes all into the old-fashioned Bertillon system of identification.

Mr. Cotten: Mr. Romanoff, were you aware of this material having been preserved by another government?

Mr. Romanoff: Yes, the statement of Mr. Herman Kimsey regarding this matter is truthful. At this point I can tell you, Mr. Cotten, that my father, His Imperial Majesty Imperator of all Russia, Nicholas II, placed in the British Trust, prior to our going into exile, certain information and proofs, including fingerprints, sole prints, pictures and some medical records for necessary identification in some critical case, so this is a fact that the C.I.A. conducted all necessary and lawful verification tests regarding my person with the aid of the British Secret Service, based in principle aspect on this material for comparison which my father placed in the British Trust. (Now at this point I wish to emphasize that the C.I.A. got some of the comparison material also from other sources.) Especially this kind of material was the principal material, and this included all of the records and conclusions and results and is the material of value just for me, because it is exclusively my private possession.

Mr. Cotten: Correct, Sir. Well, I certainly thank you for that, and if we may, now, we will turn to Mr. Kimsey and develop the nature of the documentation which was just outlined briefly and what it is you say the C.I.A. has that would establish his identity.

Mr. Kimsey: The information which we received from highly competent and qualified sources in British private investigating circles was that the British Government had issued the information to them that this material had been taken from the files of the Russian Imperial family and given to the American Intelligence Service.

Mr. Cotten: Mr. Kimsey, would you comment in depth on the affidavit of the Czarevich case?

Mr. Kimsey: Some of this material which was listed, take fingerprints for example, as was listed under Affidavit as Section A, is listed as being taken from the Czarevich in 1909. During this particular period the Czarevich was going through a considerable period of severe illness, due to his blood disease of hemophilia, and he had been taken there (England) to a specialist and during his visit there is when most of the material was solicited from him by his father, his family and medical sources, and this involved a considerable amount of medical knowledge, which is referred to further down in the listing on the affidavit. Much of this information about his medical background, his blood type, many of his peculiar facets and problems involving the under-development of his legs and feet (a problem from which he still suffers from today in a mild form), these at one time served two purposes—the information was gathered both for medical reasons and then recorded for possible future identification purposes. This apparently was a custom not unusual among Royal families of the day as they knew the possibilities of problems inherent with the overthrow and turnovers of Governments, the losses of people and memories of families. This was not an unusual thing to file such information; this was a very common thing, and had been throughout history.

Mr. Cotten: Could you say, with your experience and training with the C.I.A., that it is reasonable to assume that the documentation is more than adequate to establish his identity?

Mr. Kimsey: I would say that almost any one of the following items would be enough to substantiate the identity of this man in any Court of Law in the United States, let alone the entire list. The fingerprints alone are positive identification. The sole prints alone are positive identification. Dental charts, as listed under "C" on the affidavit, are used to identify dead bodies in almost every major disaster, this is common. These all would be accepted by Courts of Law. Blood tests of certain types, especially one so unusual and having such unusually medical relationship, this can, on occasion, become positive identification also. These are all individually quite strong enough to more than do the job.

Mr. Cotten: This, then, goes on into various medical records? You have the word "Anthropometrical" tests. What does that term mean?

Mr. Kimsey: Initially, a Belgian anthropologist in Brussels about 1832, I believe it was, discovered the fact that all human skeletons were measured differently. This was seized upon by a much harried clerk in the French Sûreté, or a man, Bertillon (as the English pronounce it). This man had been faced with the problem of trying to record the identification of criminals who were second offenders, and trying to prove that this was the same man who had been involved before, because in those days second offenders were dealt with very severely. He compiled this in a systematic form, the skeletal measurements of the human being, and he developed this into a tremendous system in which you run into breakdowns even more vast than fingerprints in number, and he was making positive identifications by comparing these measurements even at different age brackets or extended age periods. This is the basis system which, incidentally, became so cumbersome that he had to cease this and resort to a much shorter and more accurate system which is that of the artist drawing a sketch of a human face from a verbal description by a trained man.

Mr. Cotten: Mr. Kimsey, could you tell us something about your current relationship with the C.I.A. and their attitude in regard to your interest in this?

Mr. Kimsey: From the very first day I was approached by Mr. Backster to aid in this case, I went directly to the Chief of Security of the C.I.A. and I told him the situation that was developing. I voluntarily said if he could give me any adequate reason to cease and desist at any time in this investigation, if he felt that we were getting into something which was disastrous to national security in any sense of the word, we would be very happy to stop this investigation instantly. We have no desire to harm the security of the United States, and we don't want to embarrass the C.I.A. or anybody else, if this can be done. We do feel that this man's identity is something of a personal nature, that it belongs to him and no one has a right, we feel, to steal it.

Mr. Cotten: Thank you very much, Mr. Kimsey. Mr. Backster, there is a photograph that we have available, taken here in May of 1942, and I wonder if you would describe that for me please.

Mr. Backster: Yes, this photograph was taken on the occasion of the 74th birthday of Czar Nicholas II, and in May 1942, which was quite a long time after the alleged massacre. This was the first release of a photograph of Czar Nicholas II of Russia, taken 24 years after his alleged murder in 1918. The announcement and release of this photograph was made by the Academy For Scientific Interrogation Research Committee of which I am Chairman. In this photograph is pictured the Grand Duchess Maria Nikolaevna and her father the Czar, Nicholas II of Russia, and Aleksei Nikolaevich.

Mr. Cotten (Turning to Mr. Romanoff): Can you identify this picture as that of your sister, Maria?

Mr. Romanoff: Oh yes! That is my sister.

Mr. Cotten: Would you tell us who was the youngest of your sisters, Mr. Romanoff.

Mr. Romanoff: Anastasia was the youngest sister, then Maria is the second one in age and she is two years older than Anastasia who was born in 1901, and Maria was born in 1899. I was born August 12, 1904 (by the new calendar) which makes me now 62 years old as of August of this year.

Mr. Cotten: You have held your age marvelously well, and my congratulations to you!

Mr. Backster: Also released by the Research Committee of the Academy For Scientific Interrogation is the accounting of the content and photo-copies of two letters that are of quite some interest. One is a hand-written letter from the Emperor, Nicholas II of all the Russians, and dated January 6, 1919, nearly six months after the alleged death of the Emperor. Another handwritten letter was from the German Emperor, Wilhelm II, signed "Wilhelm," and the contents in these letters helped to destroy the myth of the massacre of the Russian Imperial Family. Clear photo-copies of these letters are on file with my Committee and also in proper archives are the originals of these letters.

Mr. Cotten: In other words, if and when this can be handled in the proper method to substantiate your identification, there is simply no lack of scientific documentation available.

Mr. Romanoff: Yes! I am certain that your statement regarding this matter is correct. I wish to make a statement in regard to one made by Mr. Kimsey referring especially to two points. The first point is regarding the Bertillon Method developed in 1905 by a highly classified French specialist for the identification of individual persons. By my knowledge, this method is exactly good enough as is a comparison of the finger prints, including the pictures which are substantial evidence of this method. Results of this method have already been introduced by some statements of some authorized persons, including a very important portrait painter. Now, the second problem regarding my hereditary blood disease— the expression "hemophilia" is not exactly the right expression because my hereditary blood disease is stranger i.e. more rare than hemophilia! The development of the hematology knowledge from that time 07/8/14, was going pretty quick—and even from the point of my blood disease and from some damages done by this blood disease—from his point of view there is no question that it is very definitely the right identification. No one can have the same medical records, face prints, the same finger prints, the same hereditary blood disease, the same dental charts, the same sole prints—and still be some other person.

Mr. Cotten: Is it correct that a sum of some four hundred million dollars, held in Western banks, would belong to you upon proper identification? And is it true you have stated that for the most part the money would be used in combating the International Communist Conspiracy and freeing the one billion people held in the most tyrannical rule the world has ever known?

Mr. Romanoff: Any money in deposit belongs to me or, in part, to my sisters, but you have to understand that there was approximately 400 million dollars that was deposited a long, long time ago; so, consequently, it is already now probably some billion dollars which could, in my opinion, be used to support people who are fighting for their freedom and are fighting the Bolsheviks.

Mr. Cotten: Am I correct in feeling that it would be a tremendous boon to all of those, our former allies who were so cruelly betrayed at the end of World War II, to learn of your existence? Wouldn't this be a tremendous lift to them?

Mr. Romanoff: Yes, in part I believe so. Of course, the political situation of status quo is very complicated and we have to see the matter in this complicated situation. But by all situations, it is my right that this money belongs to me as the proofs, records and conclusions in regard to the recognitions of my identity. They are of my private possession and I have the right to them here in the United States.

Mr. Cotten: May I ask in what form this substantial treasure was held and in what countries?

Mr. Romanoff: Well, it was deposited by my father in several forms. It was deposited in the Bank of England and three other banks in England as there were some deposits in money and stock in Paris and also in Germany, especially stocks in Germany. There are also stocks and money in banks in the United States, the Chase Manhattan Bank, for one. The subway which you used to reach my little apartment is a subway which in part, by stocks, belonged to me because my father many, many years ago made a deposition of capital for the development of this subway!

Mr. Cotten: Might I ask when the subways in Moscow came into being?

Mr. Romanoff: The development of the subways in Moscow came much later than that of the subway in the United States.

Mr. Cotten: Mr. Romanoff, I would think everyone would be vitally interested in the circumstances that brought you to America and your present relationship to any agency of our government and what it is you hope we can accomplish. Would you fill us in on some of this information, please?

Mr. Romanoff: Yes! It is a very complicated matter in order to give a clear picture of the whole situation and the developments during the last years. In the first place, I wish to bring to your attention the fact that after my recovery from a heavy illness, which I got during the time of imprisonment in Siberia by the Bolsheviks, and because of my hereditary blood disease, I also got malaria. This illness kept me, for probably ten years, very, very ill and in 1930 I was introduced by my father, His Imperial Majesty Emperor Nicholas II of Russia, to the All-Russian Imperial Anti-Bolshevik Movement. I was in this movement up to January 1961, at the time I was brought by authorized persons of the C.I.A. with the knowledge of Mr. Dulles, the former Director of the C.I.A. and with the knowledge of Mr. Hoover, the present Director of the F.B.I. in the United States. I arrived with my wife on January 12, 1961, by M.A.T.S. transportation via airplane at the Military Airport in Dover by Washington. From this time we have been living here in the United States.

Going back to some developments after the Second World War, I was forced to enter the Polish Army because I was poisoned in December of 1944 by some fungus bacteria. I had a very heavy operation and I was dying at this time and this part prevented my father and my sister, Maria, and myself from going out from the Western part of Poland to Portugal in order to live further there in exile in the underground before the Red Army took power all over Poland and closed the border. I never was a member of the Polish Communist Party, even by the assumed identity of Colonel Michael Goleniewski. The card membership was manipulated by some members of the All-Russian Imperial Anti-Bolshevik Underground for my cover because it was necessary. I believe that during the time from April 1958 up to December 1963, I served voluntarily with great results for the national security of this country and other allied countries in Western Europe in the fight against the Bolshevik and the Bolshevik penetrations, the KGB operations, GRU [foreign military intelligence] operations and other satellite-Red Secret Service operations. This is a matter of record of the United States Congress and in the records of the C.I.A., and the F.B.I. and other services.

Now, after living more than five years in the United States, I find myself in a very difficult situation, including my wife and my little daughter, Tatiana Alekseievna Romanoff, who is the first Tatiana, Grand Duchess of Russia born in the United States. My wife wrote an Open Letter expressing our difficulties, published by the *New York Herald Tribune* in January 1966, and by the *Washington Daily News* in February 1966, which in fact brought no change in the situation.

Mr. Cotten: This Open Letter will be included with this transcript. It is addressed to the President of the United States, Honorable Lyndon B. Johnson, and to the Speaker of the House, the Honorable John W. McCormick and to Members of the United States Congress— wherein Mrs. Romanoff outlined their present circumstances and the hardships, by virtue of Mr. Romanoff's not being able to assume his proper identity, and the fact that the C.I.A. had broken various agreements, etc.

Mr. Romanoff: I wish to emphasize without going into detail that this letter had to be set up exclusively for the purpose of the regulation of our daily lives. This Open Letter had nothing to do with my recognition as Heir Apparent, etc. It was just a matter of the proper identification cards or obligation of C.I.A. by the United States Government contract. This is very important, because during the whole six months my wife, for reason of these difficulties, became seriously ill and she is the mother of our twenty-month-old daughter. We got some nice and empty letters from some Congressmen and from the office of the Speaker of the House, Hon. McCormick. We also got a nice and empty letter from Senator Robert Kennedy, but we are still in the same, or even worse, situation than in January, 1966, before the letter from my wife appeared. We got no answer from the White House (from President Johnson), and we also sent another letter to President Johnson's personal attention regarding this matter.

Mr. Cotten: I have seen the letter from an Anti-Communist Movement here in America, an organization in Philadelphia, addressed to the President. Would you like to comment on that letter?

Mr. Romanoff: Yes! This organization is supporting me voluntarily and has been doing so for a pretty long time. They investigated my case most carefully and they spent a lot of time. I believe they were much more careful than the United States Congress, as they had the time to do so. This gentleman has already printed some statements in the American Press and sent a letter to the personal attention of the President of the United States, the Honorable Lyndon B. Johnson, regarding the release of my possessions which are proofs and verification of my identity and it was done as you can see from the letter.

Mr. Cotten: With no indication yet of any assistance?

Mr. Romanoff: No, just an acknowledgment letter from a man by the name of Mr. Watson, who is a Special Assistant to the President of the United States, but nothing else.

Mr. Cotten: We are going to need a great segment of the Nation asking that our Government substantiate this or deny it.

Robert Speller: "Czarevitch in U.S."

From *The Cincinnati Inquirer*, Friday, September 11, 1964:

The legend of the Romanov "massacre" in Ekaterinburg in July, 1918, is destroyed by the reappearance of Alexei Nikolaevich, the czarevitch, in the person of Col. Michael Goleniewski, the most important defector from Communist military ranks.

On the night of July 16--17 the Red guards in the Ipatiev House brought the imperial family downstairs into an empty room, at which point in history the events have been blurred for a variety of reasons.

According to Judge Nicholas Sokolov, who had been ordered by Admiral Kolchak and General Dietrichs of the White Russian army to investigate the strange circumstances surrounding the disappearance of the imperial family, the czar and his wife and children and four servants had been murdered.

The Sokolov investigators photographed the so-called "death chamber," which had some bullet holes and hatchet marks in the walls and floor, and blood of humans and animals splashed about. Although Sokolov was quite pessimistic that anyone could have survived such a fusillade, Pierre Gillard, former tutor of the czar's children, who viewed in person that already infamous room, doubted that such a small number of bullets could have accounted for the deaths of 11 persons.

Heeding rumors, Sokolov investigated the abandoned mines near Koptiaki, a few miles from Ekaterinburg, and there he examined the contents of the alleged burial pit.

He found Anastasia's dog Jemmy, assorted material possessions including some jewels belonging to the czar's family, eyeglasses, false teeth, one human finger and some 40 bone fragments, which he classified as mammifer [mammal] bones, unspecified as to being either human or animal.

No human skulls were found in the pit. Sokolov reported that there were insufficient bones to reconstruct even one human skeleton.

The official reaction of the Soviets to the mystery was skimpy indeed:

"The former czar will be shot. In the night of July 16, 1918, the resolution (of the Ural Soviets) was put into effect. The family of Romanov was transported to another place more secure, Signed: Bykov Sakovich, Yurovsky, et al ..."

According to the czarevitch he was given a sleeping drug by his mother, and then he, the czarina, the czar, and the Grand Duchess Marie were taken from the Ipatiev House, put on a truck and conducted out of the Ekaterinburg area by Yurovsky. Months later they reached questionable safety in Poland under the protection of Marshal Pilsudski. Olga, Tatiana and Anastasia left separately by different roads. From late 1919 until late 1960, a period of 41 years, the czarevitch lived in Poland, most of the time under the cover name of Michael Goleniewski.

It was under the latter name that U.S. Rep. Michael A. Feighan of Ohio, a close friend of the late President Kennedy, introduced a private bill in Congress (HR 5507) in the summer of last year which cleared the way for Colonial Goleniewski to become a citizen of the United States. According to the bill, "his services to the United States are rated as truly significant."

The CIA has for some reason of its own, prevented the story of the services of Colonel Goleniewski from being made public, and above all his claim to the identity of Alexei N. Romanov, only son of Czar Nicholas II.

High officials of the CIA were informed that Colonel Goleniewski was in reality the czarevitch.

When questioned by a reporter for confirmation of the czarevitch's story that he had known about, Allen Dulles, former director of the CIA, said, "It may all be true or it may not ... I do not wish to pursue the subject further."

In recent months, as the czarevitch has made attempts to bring the fact of his identity to the attention of the American people and all other people, important influences have been at work to prevent such publication. The word has gone out from Washington that Colonel Goleniewski is unreliable, is perhaps "crazy" (for whoever heard of a Polish Romanov, especially one who claims to be the czarevitch?).

The czarevitch has been examined by competent medical doctors. He has been given a clean bill of health as to his sanity and freedom from psychosis. He is suffering from a blood disease similar in effect to hemophilia, and indeed more rare. He has met with his youngest sister, the Grand Duchess Anastasia.

He has two of his other sisters ready to proclaim their own identity in the almost immediate future. Even the "doubting Thomas" will at once admit that he is a Romanov.

Appendix IV

Skulls from the "Ekaterinburg Remains"

In a complex historical and dental study published March 2, 2018, Vasily Boyko-Veliky shows that skulls from the "Ekaterinburg Remains" cannot belong to the members of the royal family.

Recently, a lot of new materials appeared in the media concerning the criminal case investigating the murder of the Royal Family. On November 27, 2017, a conference was held at the Moscow Sretensky Theological Seminary headed by Patriarch Kirill, at which experts, who were involved in the investigation, reported the interim results of their studies and examinations. However, a number of questions posed before the beginning of this scientific conference and in its course, the experts working now with the investigation, could not be answered.

One of the most critical issues is the discrepancy of the state of the teeth of skull No. 4, belonging to which by some modern researchers and the "old" consequence is attributed to Emperor Nikolai Aleksandrovich, the circumstances of the Emperor's real life. The person to whom this skull belonged suffered periodontitis (scurvy), and had untreated teeth with caries. This was noted immediately after the autopsy with the "Ekaterinburg remains" in 1991. This was written by the American researcher Charles Maples and noted experts Vyacheslav Popov and Vladimir Trezubov. The initial explanation for this discrepancy was as follows: at the beginning of the 20th century there was no anesthesia, and the Tsar allegedly was afraid to treat his teeth, despite the presence of many highly skilled dentists in Russia and Western Europe, where the Czar had repeatedly visited. Confirmation of this version was recalled by a certain Lazar Rendel, whose mother (when he was a ten-year-old boy) treated the teeth of the Emperor in Tobolsk in 1917-1918. Lazar Rendel in his memoirs sixty years later claimed that his mother allegedly told him that the Emperor had a "full mouth of rotten teeth."

Recall that by November 23, 2017, the prominent dentist Emil Aghajanyan, famous historians Leonid Bolotin and Alexei Obolensky conducted a comprehensive study of all these arguments and found that, firstly, anesthesia has been widely used since the last quarter of the XIX century, and since 1906 in Russia and other civilized countries, dentistry already widely used Novocaine—a very advanced at that time anesthetic, and now used for anesthesia in dentistry.

In a comprehensive examination of these independent specialists it was also established that the Tsar visited the dentists several times in 1910, 1914, 1917 and 1918. A total of at least 14 visits to dentists S. Kostritsky and M. Rendel had been made during the last two years of the Emperor's life.

It is also known that in the Tsarskoye Selo Alexander Palace, the seat of the Tsar's family, at the end of the 19th century, a dentist's office was equipped and, according to the financial records of the palace service, it regularly purchased a large number of exchangeable toothbrushes, powders, tooth elixirs for the members of the Tsarskoye family, carefully following the condition of their teeth.

In the examination of November 23, 2017, Lazar Rendel's memoirs were also investigated, and it was established that they were full of falsifications and sometimes almost literally repeated excerpts from M. Kasvinov's book published in 1973. It should be noted that Lazar Rendel in 1918, when the Tsar's Family was killed, was only a ten-year-old boy, and wrote his memoirs in the late 1970s, being already a 70-year old man. Actually, his memory did not retain real memory, and there were probably not many of them, so he built his "memories" mainly on the book of M. Kasvinov, and added fantasies that his father was a real state councilor and was awarded the Order of Saints Vladimir and Stanislav. Apparently, he did not expect that someone will check his memories and discover a clear discrepancy between his fantasies and actual circumstances. As is known, the list of all the gentlemen of the orders of Saints Vladimir and Stanislav is known precisely, and in them Rendel's surname does not appear. Therefore, the words that his mother Maria Rendel allegedly spoke about the state of the Emperor's teeth, do not cause any credence. Especially considering that at that time it was considered right to speak out negatively about the Emperor.

Expert opinion on November 23, 2017 was promptly commented on by prominent forensic experts Vyacheslav Popov and Vladimir Trezubov, and later anthropologist D. Pezhemsky, but in essence their objections were reduced only to the fact that there is a certain category of people who are afraid to treat their teeth, that is suffers from so-called dentophobia. According to their assumption, Emperor Nicholas II could relate to such a category of people. But "could" does not at all mean that the Emperor really belonged to such a category of patients.

V. Popov in an interview praised the historical part of the study, but noted that the dentist Emil Aghajanyan did not study the primary materials (large-scale photographs, X-rays, texts of examinations containing a description of teeth and jaw).

Responding to these objections, as well as exploring more deeply not only the published expert materials on skulls No. 4 and 7 attributed to the "old" effect of the Emperor and the Empress, but also materials on skulls No. 3, 5 and 6 attributed to the "old" consequence Cezarevnas Olga, Tatiana and Anastasia, the dentist E. Aghajanyan, together with the historians A. Obolensky and L. Bolotin, carried out a comprehensive additional examination. This examination explored in more detail the historical evidence concerning dental treatment and related other circumstances of the life of the Imperial Family, as well as the state of the teeth of skull No. 4 and responded in essence to the criticisms of V. Popov, V. Trezubov, and D. Pezhemsky.

TheTsar could not suffer with dentistry, because, firstly, there is no evidence of this, and secondly, there are precisely preserved data on his regular visits to the dentist S. Kostritsky in St. Petersburg (Petrograd) and the dentist M. Rendel in Tobolsk. The person to whom Skull No. 4 belonged also could not suffer the extreme form of dentophobia, in which there is a complete refusal of dental treatment: two of the surviving teeth of this skull have two seals, amalgam and cement, and six teeth were removed during life. In the course of an additional detailed study, it was also found out that the above-mentioned fillings in the teeth of skull No. 4 are placed extremely poorly: they protrude above the surface of the enamel, which indicates that the dental care was rendered to this person unskilled, which in no way can correspond to the qualifications of dentists.

An assertion in an interview with anthropologist V. Popov that Emperor Nicholas II went to S. Kostritsky not for the purpose of treatment, but simply to chat, as about the conversations of the Tsar and S. Kostritsky was mentioned by the chief of the guard of the Alexander Palace, General A. Spiridovich, does not stand up to any criticism.

First, there are always pauses in the treatment of teeth. The patient has to wait until the anesthesia works, while the doctor prepares some material or tools, or you should expect hardening of the filling material. And a competent doctor in such situations, as a rule, seeks to fill pauses with a secular conversation for better contact with the patient and [to] reduce his natural excitement. And S. Kostritsky was undoubtedly a competent doctor and was popular with patients and in Yalta, and after the emigration and in Paris.

Secondly, according to the financial reports of the Alexander Palace for a visit to a dental chair to S. Kostritsky each of the members of the royal family paid their personal money, including the Emperor. Is it possible to imagine that for happiness it is only to talk with S. Kostritsky, did the Tsar pay him 200 rubles in January 1917? Rather, on the contrary: many subjects were willing to spend money for the happiness of being at the Tsar's reception. It is clear that the Emperor paid for his own dental treatment from the doctor S. Kostritsky.

Thirdly, what about the dentist Maria Rendel, the sympathizing party of the Socialist-Revolutionaries? Was she specifically summoned to the house of the Tobolsk Governor, where the Tsar's Family lived in 1917-1918, for a conversation with the Emperor, and not for treatment?

A textual analysis of the records in the diaries of the Emperor indicates that it is a question of treatment, and not just conversations. Often used in the diary of the Emperor, the word sat in relation to the stay, and from S. Kostritsky and M. Rendel related precisely to the stay—sitting in a dental chair in both doctors.

For memories of communicating with S. Kostritsky, the words of the Emperor indicate the presence of communication with the treating doctor on the background of treatment, while for the stay in the armchair of the revolutionary-minded Maria Rendel, the Emperor had only one definition—sitting, clearly reflecting the essence of his presence in her office rather than the treatment of teeth.

In many other diary entries of the Sovereign it is directly stated that he "spoke", "told" this or that to some person, and not "sat". The definition of "sitting" we never see (!) in the Emperor's records relating to any other situations, except those described above with regard to S. Kostritsky and M. Rendel.

Thus, the version of "conversations with the dentist and dentist" instead of treatment does not find its objective confirmation. More on this in the article by A. Obolensky (What did the Emperor Nicholas II do for dentists?).

Another circumstance was also revealed: six teeth removed from the owner of skull No. 4, two teeth (sixth and eighth) were removed 2-3 months before death (experts determine this by the degree of overgrowth of the hole). The sixth tooth is much more difficult to remove, in addition, the owner of the skull No. 4 developed acute osteomyelitis before the removal of this tooth, that is, the purulent inflammation of the periosteum, which caused this person to have severe pain and practically eliminated the possibility of chewing on the affected side of the jaw. The extremely painful condition had a considerable duration after removal of the tooth, which required continued treatment. Undoubtedly, such pains and associated consequences would affect the everyday behavior of a person and would be obvious to others. These visual features of the behavior and its consequences would be reflected either in the diary of the Emperor himself, or in the diary of the Tsaritsa, where even the illnesses of the confidants are mentioned, or in the certificates of Doctor Derevenko who visited prisoners in the Ipatiev house, or in the testimonies of regicides. There is no such evidence, which means that there was no natural reason for such evidence.

It is known that the Emperor Nikolai Alexandrovich stayed about 3 months before the villainous murder in the "House of Special Appointment" in Ekaterinburg, in the so-called Ipatiev House, in which the journal of visits was conducted. The Emperor and the Empress themselves kept diaries and correspondences with people close to them. And according to these documents it can be seen that there were no visits to dentists who could remove the teeth from the Emperor, there was no Ipatiev house. And moreover, the Sovereign did not experience any dental pain at that time. Yes, and in Tobolsk in April 1918 before leaving for Ekaterinburg on April 26 and on the road no visit of the Imperial Family to the dentist was recorded, in contrast to March 1918. The last visit of the dentist Maria Rendel was March 3, 1918, according to a new calendar style, that is, four and a half months before the villainous murder.

The Empress Alexandra Feodorovna carefully noted in her diaries the illnesses of all the members of the Royal Family and even the illness of Dr. E. Botkin, who at that time suffered from kidney colic and spent all May in bed. Spells and illness of Dr. E. Botkin the Empress describes in her diary in detail, but does not write anything about any illness of the Emperor, who, according to her records and according to his own diary, led a normal way of life, eating without the slightest inconvenience in the usual way, as far as possible, [for] physical exercise, went out into the cold (April and May in both Ekaterinburg and Tobolsk—very cool, people go [in] their coats), that with osteomyelitis and strong toothaches, of course, it would be absolutely impossible.

In general, the presence of multiple untreated caries, periodontitis, and osteomyelitis should have caused a putrid smell from the mouth of the owner of skull No. 4. But even the royalists never noted such a thing in the Emperor.

The assertion of the anthropologist D. Pezhemsky about the dental status of the skull No. 4 is verbatim: the person has few teeth left. After the death of the owner of skull No. 4, slightly more than half of the teeth were lost, but the remaining half, as we see from professional expertise, is enough to make an unambiguous conclusion that skull No. 4 could not belong to the Emperor.

The teeth in skull No. 7, attributed to the "old" effect of the Empress, were subjected to serious and careful treatment, which is quite affordable for people of a wealthy circle. The owner of this skull had prostheses, crowns made of porcelain, gold and platinum, there were seals, teeth that had been removed during life. But at the time of death, the owner of the skull number 7 had 14 untreated carious cavities that had not undergone any treatment and 3 recurring caries under the seals! On one of the teeth there was pulpitis, that is, it rotted from the inside. In addition, the teeth of the skull number 7 are prone to severe periodontitis and they have numerous granulomas. The owner of the skull number 7, too, with such teeth was supposed to have a putrid odor from her mouth.

It is impossible to imagine that Empress Alexandra Feodorovna, attentively following behind the Emperor and the children, had visibly rotten teeth. Such conditions are associated with lack of dental care, with improper and inadequate nutrition and lack of vitamins (scurvy), which, of course, there was not in the Tsar's family, and could not be. Even in Ekaterinburg from April 30 to July 16—almost to the most villainous murder—the Emperor and the Empress received a relatively normal diet for 78 days, not to mention the times when they were imprisoned in the Tsarskoe Selo Alexander Palace and then in Tobolsk. Nobody ever said that the Emperor or the Empress had a bad smell from her mouth.

As already mentioned above, the Royal Family used the services of many dentists. In the last few years, before their martyrdom, it was mostly Dr. S. Kostritsky, who lived and worked in Yalta and specially came to Tsarkoye Selo to treat the Empress, the Emperor and the Tsar's Children. In the following brief reference, the exact dates for visiting the members of the Royal Family by the dentist S. Kostritsky, who came even to Tobolsk in October 1917, are specified. Later, the Emperor used the services of a local dentist Maria Rendel, as mentioned above. The same doctor could [be used by] the Empress. Thus, it is absolutely impossible to imagine the presence in the Tsarina Alexandra Feodorovna of 14 untreated carious cavities.

Approximately the same can be said about girls who owned skulls 3, 5 and 6. In one of them, as can be seen from the table, there are 9 primary carious cavities, in the other 8, in the third 4, and already recurring caries and more: 10, 16 and 19 respectively. And all three had periodontitis in their initial form. This does not fit in any way with the image of tsarinas, who worked as nurses during the war and also closely followed their teeth and visited dentists, although much less frequently than the Emperor and the Empress. What is natural, young girls' teeth, of course, are in a better condition than their parents.

In the complex additional expertise of February 8, 2018, specialists E. Agadzhanyan, L. Bolotin [and] A. Obolensky also established that the skull No. 2 could not belong to Dr. E. Botkin because its owner shortly before his death (for a 1.5-2 months) removed two teeth. Neither in the diaries of the Sovereign and the Empress, nor in the preserved correspondence, nor in the journal of visits to the "House of Special Appointment" does it mention that it was at the time when E. Botkin suffered from kidney colic and lay in bed that someone was removing his aching teeth! If in Tobolsk E. Botkin was still allowed to walk around the city, then in Ekaterinburg, where he was from April 30, he was at liberty but did not go out and could not visit the dentist. There are other grounds, stated in the examination, why this skull could not belong to Dr. E. Botkin.

We will not retell the entire contents of the multi-page review from February 8, 2018. You can find it on the website of the *Moscow Gazette*.

It is possible, of course, to continue research into the "Ekaterinburg remains", but even carrying out a genetic examination (which is of a probabilistic nature) with a positive result cannot undo the results of a comprehensive historical dental examination, which unambiguously indicate that the skull from the "Ekaterinburg remains" could not belong to the Emperor, the Empress, the three Tsarinas and the doctor E. Botkin. It is quite obvious that people whose remains were buried in the so-called Porosencov Log, for the past year or two, and maybe even three years of their life, they have not eaten well, could not take care of their teeth, did not receive proper dental care, except for the removal of teeth from two people (skull No. 2 and No. 4) shortly before death. This could be due to the fact that all these people in the last years of life, perhaps, were in prison, in a concentration camp or in exile in a remote village where dentists were absent. These people lacked quality food [and] vitamins. The results of the independent historical and dental examinations show the irreconcilable discrepancy between the dental status of the "Ekaterinburg remains" and the possible condition of the teeth of the members of the Royal Family.

The question arises: why is this examination carried out only now, because the description of the teeth of skulls from the so-called Porosencov Log was known to the old investigation in the 1990s. The answer is simple. Back in 1998, at a conference in Tsarkoye Selo, Professor Alexander Bastrykin (now head of the Investigative Committee of Russia) described how the literary style of the investigator V. Soloviev's work was illiterate and pointed to his main mistakes: the lack of comprehensive and historical expertise, which are now held in the part of comparing the dental status of skulls from the "Ekaterinburg remains" and historical evidence of dental treatment of the Imperial Family.

Thus, it is necessary to return to the resolution of the Synod of the Russian Orthodox Church from 1998, which says that the "Ekaterinburg remains" must be buried in a separate grave with the inscription "Their names, Lord, You are the weights". We do not know and are unlikely to know who these people were when they died or were killed, but the Lord knows their names, like the names of all the millions of sufferers who died in the fratricidal and bloody turmoil that followed the villainous murder of the Holy Family.

Harry Binkow's comments on the above article, written in an email:

On Sun, Mar 18, 2018 at 9:08 AM, Harry Binkow <harrybinkow@ gmail.com> wrote:

Another comprehensive article from February 24, 2018 verifying what we already knew. Those are not the remains of any of the Imperial Family of Russia, supposedly killed in July 1918.

All of you have been informed years ago that the work performed on any remains involving DNA evidence to the lineage of Tsar Nicholas II and his family was obviously compromised. We also know the very reasons and have complete documented evidence from many royals who continued their relationships with all of them.

From the Russian Imperial Historical Society

This article by the Russian Imperial Historical Society was written in 2013.

All four daughters of Nicholas and Alexandra survived the Russian revolution and were evacuated from Russia. They lived in different countries under false identities.

The treaty of Brest Litovsk granted their freedom. Other members of the Romanov Family also escaped thanks to that agreement.

The truth of this story is that Tsarina and her children were transferred to Perm on the night of July 16/17 1918. They were not murdered.

Sir Charles Eliot, British High Commissioner and Consul General in Siberia, one of the two highest ranking diplomats in Russia, a man of extraordinary culture, sent with the precise instruction to see with his own eyes and to give his own opinion on [the] trend of things, investigating the massacre, sent in code [his] first cable in London to the [foreign secretary] Balfour, reporting:

"The mystery surrounds the fate of the tsars, which according to the Bolsheviks [were] shot here on the night of July 16, while some of the highest-ranking and best informed officials are convinced that His Imperial Majesty was not killed but taken away and given in custody of the Germans, and that the story of the murder was then invented to explain [his] disappearance. The official in charge of the current government (the Whites) to investigate the crime showed me the house where the imperial family was locked up and where His Imperial Majesty is said to have been shot. He rejected (Sergeev) as frames all the stories concerning the discovery of the corpses, and the confessions of the soldiers who would participate in the execution … It is a general opinion that the empress, the son and the four daughters were not killed but transferred, on 17 July, to the north or west. The story that [has] them burned in a quarry seems to be an amplification of the fact that a pile of ash was found, a clear remnant of a large pile of clothes. At the bottom of the ashes there was a diamond … and since it is said that one of the grand duchesses had sewn a diamond in the lining of [her] dress, it was believed that the bodies of the imperial family were burned here.

"On 17 July a train with the curtains down departed from Ekaterinburg for an unknown destination: it is believed that members of the imperial family were on board. It therefore seems probable that the imperial family disguised itself before the departure.

"In Perm they were held captives by the Cheka, while the Germans, the Vatican, and King Alfonso XIII [of Spain] were negotiating their liberation. King Alfonso sent to Perm a medical contingent to examine the imperial prisoners. There exist 4 reports (2 dated in September and 2 in October 1918), signed by the chief doctor about the physical and mental condition of Tsarina Alexandra Feodorovna and two Grand Duchesses. THEY WERE ALIVE!

"Even the newspapers in Spain were reporting about the visit of the medical team to Russia, to examine the prisoners. But some pseudo historians still claim that Alfonso XIII was "fooled" by the Bolsheviks. Not true!

"The King of SPAIN participated adamantly in the negotiations. He sent his own representative to Moscow to talk with Chicherin and Radek, not once but twice and obtained the invaluable help of his relatives in Austria. He was aware of every single detail of the negotiations and helped them while the Romanov women were in exile. All his family knew about the survival of Nicholas' family. His son Don Juan of Bourbon did the same. He visited Olga in Italy. There is A LOT in this story that still needs to be told."

The Bacha List

Tsarevich Alexi Harry is said to be buried outside the St. Alexander Nevsky Cathedral in Serbia. He was given a different name and worked for the United Nations.

Harry Binkow states that Tsarina Alexandra was then rescued after the royal family's alleged assassination in a Catholic Monastery in Lviv.

Mother Alexandra as Princess Ileana was a planned conception at the time of the wedding of Maria Pavlovna.

St. Elizabeth, the Granduchess Sege, or as Mother Alexandra would call her, "Aunt Ella," arranged for the union of Nicholas II and Queen Marie when Tsarina Alexandra did not attend the wedding.

So Princess Ileana, Mother Alexandra, is the blood daughter of Tsar Nicholas II and Queen Marie of Romania.

In my single adulthood when I spent months at a time with Mother Alexandra we then had the rug given her by Tsar Nicholas II as the chapel rug we knelt down on.

In the dining room at Transfiguration Monastery there were the dishes given to the princess by Tsar Nicholas. They were on a display shelf at that time.

Mother Alexandra had a nun then my age Sister Catherine, now Mother Cassiana in Colorado, who was very vehemently opposed to any talk of Mother Alexandra's past history.

So, I would be then in Mother Alexandra's private company at her then retreat house to help her document and discuss important features she wanted me to carry on as "Aunt Ella." She prepared me to be the Abbess of the Transfiguration Monastery.

This was all before the time of Mother Christophora. Later Mother Christophora would come after being a parishioner in Harrisburg,

Pennsylvania, and getting support from this parish where I had taken Mother Alexandra for the first time in October of 1974 or 1975.

At the time of my second pregnancy, Mother Alexandra sent me the special icon given to her mother Queen Marie by Tsar Nicholas II, when I was ill at my parents' home in greater Harrisburg while my then husband Theodore Bacha continued his seminary studies at St. Tikhon's.

That icon was a small silver two-sided locket with St. Barbara on one side and the other side the Face of Christ on the cross-stitched towel.

I was able to communicate with Patriarch Alexei II on some of these issues as well as on his visit to Miami in November of 1992.

Romania held Orthodoxy as the standard. Many times I heard Mother Alexandra explain to people how she became Orthodox by virtue of the Romanian state decree. How her parents were brought in as rulers and peacekeepers for this smaller country but for her baptism she was to be Orthodox.

Faith and country were central to organizing this "kingdom on earth to prepare for the heavenly kingdom," but faith in one God, Father, Son and Holy Spirit were the central focus to the leadership she was formed to assume.

When all Europe was in post-war turmoil, Queen Marie's vision of the trip to America organized by Sam Hill and the blessing for the peace arch between the US and Canada by her the Queen held out hope that America would be a partner to this aid and the transformation of Romania as well as the larger world.

As Princess Ileana, now in a car in America working to pay her bills by speaking, writing and promoting her book ... In the 1950s she hoped this vision to defeat Communism as the ideology would materialize.

Princess Ileana's monastic formation was as strong as ever as she negotiated driving across America fueled by the earlier 1926 train travel with her beloved mother, Queen Marie.

Building Community as Christians to help one another and reflecting on Ron Dreher's "Benedict Option" is what she passed on for me to do in the manner of "Aunt Ella."

Those who are "out" [unpopular] in the worldly sense [this could be in the Church] may be the ones closest to our Lord as He was OUT for the dominant religious group of his day.

The bigger point out of Queen Marie's 1926 trip financed by Sam Hill (hence the expression "What the Sam Hill are you doing?") was to get American investment in Romanian coal, oil and gas and to get out of the Soviet claws by showing Queen Marie as the peacemaker.

The train trip was to include the south and to Orlando, Florida. There in Orlando in advance of the tour, a street was named for Ileana. Just as in her trip to Cuba a third of the population named their child Ileana after the beautiful young daughter they saw with Queen Marie.

As I mentioned before, life with Mother Alexandra when I was 19-20 years old was better than my first year in college at Indiana University of Pennsylvania, IUP. We were like college roommates. Age was not a factor.

When she was a teenager, Princess Ileana was teaching Bible stories to the summer shepherd boys, the 4 Ions (Ioans), who were the Romanov family members.

She went to the microwave when not eating what they served in the dining room. She was not a fan of seeing Sister Catherine's tuna salad reappear at a 2nd or 3rd lunch. She had lunch with the sisters, dinner on her own when I was there.

Mother Alexandra: no high school diploma; above-average intelligence; IQ in the 125 to 140 range; hearing affected mildly from bombing re auditory processing. She excelled at embroidery and drawing and painting.

She liked chocolates.

Her cats: Peepers and Elsa. The bigger orange and white cat, Peepers, was the hunter. When she would be away any length of time, Peepers would bring into the basement of the retreat house some rodent prize offering.

She was the first to recognize my goiter and sent me to her doctor. Start of my thyroid condition.

She bought the special bed with me on our Pittsburgh outing. She needed the angled head up. She had trouble swallowing. There was a problem with [the] esophagus.

She enjoyed my salmon pie. Lazy pirogues, vegetable borscht.

One of her favorite foods: Stouffer's frozen spinach soufflé.

Peepers the cat was [the] "man of the house." While in bed, Peepers would lie by her shoulders and gently take his paw with no claws to stroke her cheek and make those affectionate cat communiqués.

Appendix VII

Bullet Biography

Born on January 5, 1909 in Bucharest, Romania's capital. Princess Ileana was the youngest daughter of King Ferdinand I and Princess Marie of Edinburgh, who was the granddaughter of Queen Victoria of England and first cousin to Empress Alexandra of Russia.

As a young child Princess Ileana met and befriended the children of the last Russian Tsar, Nicholas II, who were her second cousins. She became especially fond of Tsarevich Alexei, heir to the throne of Russia. Both sets of parents did not exclude the possibility of marriage between their children some time in the future; Alexei's eldest sister—Grand Duchess Olga—was also thought to have been a good dynastic match for Ileana's older brother Carol, heir to the Romanian throne.

The possibility of any Russian marriages ended with the reported brutal murder of the entire Romanov family in 1918.

As a teenager and young woman, Ileana was the leader of the Romanian Young Women's Red Cross Reserve, and later founded the first social work school in Romania.

She was an avid sailor. She could navigate competently and had sailed the ship *Isprava* for many years.

On July 26, 1931, Ileana married Archduke Anton of Austria, Prince of Tuscany. King Carol II, Ileana's brother, wanted this marriage. He was very jealous of Ileana's popularity in Romania, and wanted her out of the country. After his sister's wedding, Carol announced that the Romanian people would never tolerate the Habsburgs on Romanian territory. Ileana and Anton were pressured to leave Romania.

After the newlywed royal couple arrived in the bride's new country, the Archduchess Ileana became president of the Austrian Young Women Guides.

During World War Two, after her husband was drafted into the German Air Force, Ileana founded a hospital for the wounded Romanian soldiers at their castle, Sonneburg.

In 1944, Ileana and her children returned to Romania, where they lived in Bran Castle, near Brasov. Archduke Anton later joined them, but was placed under house arrest by the Red Army. Princess Ileana worked at another hospital in the village of Bran, which she named "The Queen of Hearts" as a tribute to her mother, Queen Marie.

Ileana and her husband were largely estranged when she had an affair with one of the local senior communist officials, who helped her keep her hospital open. But by late 1947, this was no longer possible and Ileana was told that she and her family had to leave the new communist Romania.

They eventually settled in Switzerland, then moved to Argentina, and in 1950 Ileana and her children moved to the United States and settled in Newton, Massachusetts.

In 1954, Ileana and Anton officially divorced, and later that year she got married for the second time to Dr. Stefan Nicolaus Issarescu.

In 1961, Princess Ileana decided to enter the Convent of the Intercession of the Mother of God in Bussy, France, where she was given the name Alexandra. Ileana's second marriage ended in official divorce a few years later.

Sister Alexandra returned to the United States and founded the Orthodox Monastery of the Transfiguration in Ellwood City, Pennsylvania. She served there as an abbess until her retirement in 1981, remaining at the convent for the rest of her life.

She always spelled Ellwood with one "l."

Ileana had the chance to return to Romania in 1990 at the age of 81, along with her daughter. Early the following year she fell and broke her hip, consequently suffering two heart attacks at the hospital.

Afterword

Aleksandr Solzhenitsyn and Communism

Sometime in the late 1980s, a Boston friend of mine brought up the books of Aleksandr Solzhenitsyn. I had never read any of Solzhenitsyn's works but I was aware that he was the author of *The Gulag Archipelago*, *Cancer Ward*, and *One Day in the Life of Ivan Denisovich*, and that he was awarded the Nobel Prize for Literature in 1970.

For a good many years, Solzhenitsyn's works had nothing to say to me. I was more interested in Susan Sontag's critiques of art and culture; in Paul Goodman's diary, Five Years; in Gore Vidal's caustic, pagan wit; in Edmund White's Parisian stories; and in Christopher Isherwood's Berlin of the 1930s. The works of Edmund Wilson, Mary McCarthy, and Henry Miller also filled my library shelves.

The unkempt-looking Solzhenitsyn was, to my mind, too Russian. According to my Boston friend, Solzhenitsyn was also "too conservative … a real reactionary." Solzhenitsyn's critics, including *The Boston Globe*, accused him of wanting to revive the Russian Orthodox monarchy and resented his harsh criticisms of the West.

"Hastiness and superficiality are the psychic disease of the 20th century and more than anywhere else this disease is reflected in the press," Solzhenitsyn said at Harvard University's 327th Commencement ceremony in 1978.

Such as it is, however, the press has become the greatest power within the Western countries, more powerful than the legislative power, the executive, and the judiciary. And one would then like to ask: By what law has it been elected and to whom is it responsible? Who has granted Western journalists their power, for how long a time, and with what prerogatives?

The "press problem" of course has multiplied exponentially since the author's death in 2008.

Solzhenitsyn, the prophet, also stated:

I have received letters in America from highly intelligent persons, maybe a teacher in a faraway small college who could do much for the renewal and salvation of his country, but his country cannot hear him because the media are not interested in him. This gives birth to strong mass prejudices, to blindness, which is most dangerous in our dynamic era.

Solzhenitsyn's Harvard address established him as an arch enemy of liberal academics, some of whom even accused him of anti-Semitism. Solzhenitsyn, who spent eight years in a forced labor camp under the old Soviet regime because he criticized Josef Stalin in a personal letter, heaps many other criticisms of the West in his memoir, *Between Two Millstones*, Book 2, "Exile in America, 1978-1994," by University of Notre Dame Press.

"Current literature in the West," he wrote, "titillates either an intellectual or a popular readership: it is degraded to the level of entertainment and paradox, no longer of a standard to mold minds and characters."

He also observed that when he was serving his time in the camps, still under Stalin, he imagined Russian literature after communism to be "Luminous, skillful, powerful ... dealing with the ills of the people and all the suffering since the Revolution!" Yet once the post-Soviet "emancipated literature" came pouring forth, Russia's new West-inspired authors behaved like "mischievous little boys using their first taste of freedom to pick up swear words in the gutter," while other writers went for no-holds-barred sex.

A third group opted for self-expression:

A buzzword and the supreme vindication of their literary activity. What a pathetic principle. "Self-expression" does not presuppose self-restraint, either in society or before God. And is there in fact anything to express?

Solzhenitsyn felt that the American press was cut from the same cloth.

Articles were constantly appearing in *The New York Times* and its supplements, and in other major papers, saying that Russian national consciousness now being reborn consisted above all of anti-Semitism—which meant it was worse than any Communism.

The *Washington Post* at the time even published a cartoon entitled "the Virgin of Vladimir," with a hammer and sickle on her forehead, with the caption, "Mother Russia."

Some American critics even said that the rebirth of Orthodoxy in Russia was like the Islamic Revolution in Iran.

The New York Review of Books, like *The London Review of Books*—two publications that only review books that meet their strict leftist standards—were also on Solzhenitsyn's tail. In 1979, this fact was apparent to Solzhenitsyn, who labeled the NYRB, "the stronghold of American radicalism." The NYRB published a cover story entitled, "The Dangers of Solzhenitsyn's Nationalism" and hinted that the former Gulag slave labor prisoner was a fascist.

Winston S. Churchill wrote in a 1937 essay:

Nazism and Communism imagine themselves as exact opposites. They are at each other's throats wherever they exist all over the world. They actually breed each other; for the reaction against Communism is Nazism, and beneath Nazism or Fascism Communism stirs convulsively.

To this day, Russia-hating among Americans has a long legacy quite apart from the evils rampant in the now-gone Soviet Union.

Solzhenitsyn writes:

The Russia- haters are already sinking their teeth into Russia's good name. And what would happen later, when we crawled out, weak, infirm, from under the ruins of the hateful Bolshevik empire? They wouldn't even let us start getting back on our feet.

The new Russian nationalists after the fall of the Soviet Union condemned Christianity, saying that it blunted the combative spirit and that it was "Judaism's Trojan Horse."

"Russia has been slandered for centuries," Solzhenitsyn continues. "Repent? We certainly have things to repent of—we've committed enough sins!—but it's not to biased American journalism that we must repent."

World forces aligned themselves against the Russian writer, especially when he migrated to the United States and took up residence in Vermont with his wife, Natalya Svetlova, and their three sons.

Norman Podhoretz, editor for many years of *Commentary*, came to Solzhenitsyn's defense when he wrote. "In my opinion, Solzhenitsyn's evident bitterness over the fact—and it is of course a fact—that revolutionaries of Jewish origin played so important a role in bringing Communism to Russia is overridden by his consistently fervent support of Israel."

The *Boston Globe* called Solzhenitsyn "a brooding apocalyptic presence" when it was supposed that the author had taken control of a "network of radio stations in Russia." What did not help Solzhenitsyn was the fact that he was favored by President Ronald Reagan. Critics called him a Russian ultranationalist ("fascist scum ... financed by Hitler"). Once again, he was labeled an anti-Semite. That label and other heavy-handed virtue-signaling was enough to arouse the curiosity of Washington politicians. The Senate Committee on Foreign Relations soon established a Hearing.

"American senators and congressmen like nothing better than to sit at microphones, on lofty platforms, brows sternly knit, and display their uncommon perceptiveness and superior intellect," Solzhenitsyn wrote.

As it turned out, the Hearing came to nothing. It was merely an early form of Russiagate, the conspiracy theory that became the rage after the 2016 U.S. elections. The author, in addressing the issue, wrote that the anti-Semitism label "like other labels, lost its precise meaning due to thoughtless use, and different social and political commentators over the decades have understood a variety of different things by it."

Solzhenitsyn recalls an interview with CBS's Mike Wallace: "Mike Wallace asked dull and then vile questions—still the same well-oiled refrain that had been running for decades."

Forbes magazine was fair to him in its reporting and editorials, but during his life a number of biographies appeared that skirted the bastion of truth and took many things he said out of context, or otherwise presented false narratives. Solzhenitsyn even had difficulty within the USSR during the Glasnost period. "During these final years of thaw in the USSR," he wrote, "they had managed to publish all the banned authors who'd died, and all the banned ones still living—all except me."

For the remainder of his life, the Russian writer reaffirmed the themes in his great Harvard Address of 1978.

For a refugee from communist Romania in 1978, Solzhenitsyn's Harvard address changed his life. Sergiu Klainerman wrote in *Crisis of Faith* in 2020:

> When I first heard this speech in 1978 as a young refugee from communist Romania, I was able to appreciate Solzhenitsyn's address in terms of the competition raging then between the West and the East, but did not comprehend its larger meaning. Rereading it today, in the fall of the horrible year 2020, I find it truly prophetic. It is now painfully clear that, as Solzhenitsyn was able to discern 42 years ago, the West has been gradually losing the will and intellectual ability to defend itself, not so much against foreign armies as it may have appeared in 1978, but against an army of internal critics determined to demolish everything the West used to stand for.

In 1994, he returned to his native (post-communist) Russia. He died in 2008. "Aleksandr Solzhenitsyn, the celebrated Russian writer, has been laid to rest after a funeral service held at Moscow's historic Donskoy monastery earlier today," *The Guardian* reported.

Solzhenitsyn's Philadelphia connection resides in the life and career of his middle son, Ignat, who is currently Conductor Laureate of the Chamber Orchestra of Philadelphia.

Bibliography

Alexandra, Mother, *The Holy Angels* (Chesterton, IN: Ancient Faith Publishing, 2019)

Bloy, Leon, *The Desperate Man* (Snuggle Books, 2020)

Brewster, Ralph H., *The 6,000 Beards of Athos* (New York: D. Appleton-Century Company, 1936)

Chatwin, Bruce, *Under the Sun, The Letters of Bruce Chatwin* (New York: Penguin Group, 2010)

Cooke, Bev, *Royal Monastic: Princess Ileana of Romania, The Story of Mother Alexandra* (Chesterton, IN: Ancient Faith Publishing, 2008)

d'Herbigny, Michel, *Vladimir Soloviev, A Russian Newman* (Chattanooga: Catholic Resources, 2015)

Edwards, Tudor, *Worlds Apart: A Journey to the Great Living Monasteries of Europe* (New York: Coward-McCann, Inc., 1958)

Ferro, Marc, *Nicholas II, The Last of the Tsars* (New York, Oxford: Oxford University Press, 1990)

Gress, Carrie, *The End of Woman: How Smashing the Patriarchy Has Destroyed Us* (Washington, D.C.: Regnery Publishing, 2023)

Hennessy, James-Pope, *The Quest for Queen Mary* (London: Zuleika, 2018)

Hinshaw, Daniel B., *Journey to Simplicity: The Life and Wisdom of Archimandrite Roman Braga* (Yonkers, New York: St. Vladimir's Seminary Press, 2023)

Howorth, Peter, and Thomas, Christopher, *Encounters on the Holy Mountain: Stories from Mount Athos* (Turnhout, Belgium: Brepols Publishers, 2020)

Ileana, Princess of Romania, Archduchess of Austria, *I Live Again* (New York: Rinehart & Company, Inc., 1951)

Keysor, Joseph, *Against Feminism* (USA: Suzeteo Enterprises, 2012)

Maritain, Jacques, *The Primacy of the Spiritual* (Providence, Rhode Island: Cluny, 2020)

Merton, Thomas, *Turning Toward the World: The Journals of Thomas Merton, 1960–63* (San Francisco: Harper, 1996)

Mindszenty, Jozsef Cardinal, *Memoirs* (San Francisco: Ignatius Press, 2023)

Pakula, Hannah, *The Last Romantic, A Biography of Queen Marie of Romania* (London: Weidenfeld & Nicolson, 1985)

Petrov, Vadim, *The Escape of Alexei, Son of Tsar Nicholas II: What Happened the Night the Romanov Family Was Executed* (New York: Harry N. Abrams, Inc., 1998)

Ryden, Vassula, *Heaven Is Real But So Is Hell* (New York, Bath: Alexian Limited, 2013)

Smith, Douglas, *Rasputin: Faith, Power, and the Twilight of the Romanovs* (New York: Farrar, Straus and Giroux, 2016)

Soloviev, Vladimir, *Russian and The Universal Church* (Chattanooga: Catholic Resources, 1913)

Solzhenitsyn, Aleksandr, *The Red Wheel*, March 1917, Node III, Book 4 (Notre Dame, IN: University of Notre Dame Press, 2024)

Sontag, Susan, *On Women* (New York: Farrar, Straus and Giroux, 2023)

Trufanoff, Sergei (Iliodor), *The Mad Monk of Russia* (New York, The Century Company, 1918)